Contents

ON THE COVER:
CUSTOMS AND ROADSTERS... Just like the old days only better, right, yea much better.

www.hopupmag.com

HOP UP CONTRIBUTORS

MARK MORTON — Publisher/Editor, JAY WARD — Managing Editor

MARC D'ESTOUT — Art Direction/Design/Production

DERBY AHLSTONE, RICK AMADO, HERBERT BLOMQUEST, DAVID BROST, JACK BUTLER, ART CHRISMAN, JON GOBETTI, JOHN GUNSAULIS, DREW HARDIN, JEZ HOYE, NEAL JENNINGS, ED JUSTICE Jr., ERIC LOE, NORM MARCHMENT, SPENCER MURRAY, MIKE NARCISO, CURTIS PATIENCE, BRETT REED, COY THOMAS, TIM THOMPSON, PETER VINCENT, CHUCK VRANAS, BUCKSHOT WILKINS

S0-ARG-241

Mort's Shorts

It's like a séance: We queue up here every year to receive spiritual communication from our antecedents. You know, those guys whose lives were – from what we've seen – spent in black and white, wrangling for gow on dusty panoramic moonscapes and in front of pre-war houses with grey lawns and dank garages...or on the street...and, inevitably...in our imaginations.

We revere those cats; we emulate them and, since we are predisposed to nostalgic notions when we engage their grey and sepia images, it feels right. Makes us wanna be there, listen, find out what the chat sounded like, hear the cackle outta those pipes, and see if it smelled gassy and oily like it does when we do it in Hopupland.

And then? Then...we get to respond.

The topic is your gow job, your tail-dragger, your racer...and ours. The roles reverse and now we're communicatin' with them. Oh yeah, buddy, they receive as well as send. Those spirits are ambidextrous, and the dialogue is about trad hot rods with no cultural flair. It's about customs with no social mandate to be from a certain city or club. It's about the iron, and as you know, you could do it in a vacuum; might even prefer it that way. It requires depth. Focus. Resistance to trend.

We think that while we praise our predecessors, the communication between you and them is correspondence between peers. Oh, yeah: their counterparts are among us, equals in many ways and sometimes the modern trad guy may be more skilled, better equipped and equally purposeful. It looks easier for our guys because of the trinkets of modern convenience we enjoy, from tools to books to internet access and air conditioned shops.

Hot Rod Séance

Let there be no doubt: our gang's got the stuff.

Point is, here, m' man, that we got it very good; certainly better than they had it. But there is some risk that, given the social/political environment and the environment itself...we could be legislated out of business – not today – but without question within the time of the youngest Greasers. This could eventually prove to have been the perfect time to have indulged this stuff...without the hardships of the early 1900s and without the possible assassination of the concept during the new millennium.

Let's hope that our modest numbers cause us to be a 'novelty without consequence' to the politicos and not an easy target for zealous over-reaction.

It'd be a shame if, when we Greybeards are gone, we don't have anybody to talk to.

True to Tradition

VINTAGE AIR

1976 - 2008

A Hot Rod Tradition

CROCKETT HOTEL

THIRTY TWO

Since the day we created the world's first performance air conditioning system 32 years ago, every Vintage Air system has been ours from start to finish. When you choose to use a Vintage Air system you're getting the very best of everything we have learned as the oldest and most respected name in the business.

800.862.6658   www.vintageair.com

Hot Rods

When we claim traditional **foundings,** well...We mean it.

In an almost static art form, we report on new projects done by old, traditional means. We show old projects rescued from oblivious storage, and we feature old cars restored or even just resuscitated back to a state of usable iron.

We're surfing a retro wave (maybe Hop Up was one of the small earthquakes that helped induce the tsunami) so there are plenty of subjects out there. Lots to chew on. **Options**, Baby. Yeah, options that lead to **selectivity**. But it isn't the best of the best, or the 'pick'. Hop Up feature cars are usually the kind that might be found in your garage or mine; they're the kind that have style and soul, transcending trend and locking their images into our grey matter. What we got here is what catches the eye, selected because we might not have seen it anywhere else. They'll have attributes that reinforce your own sensible hot rod style.

What with the instant coverage we get on the internet, and a proliferation of tradition in print, if we're gonna be current, we have to look under a rock here and there. We have to **divine** our way around looking for that thoughtful, **considered** expression of hot rod art that might not have been covered everywhere already. So we do that in a hot rod, travelin', prowlin', snoopin', and comin'-a-callin' sort of way.

So keep an ear to the ground...watch that bit o' road...you know...where the State Highway dumps on to Main Street? The **'Divining Rod'** may drive into your town right after the thaw...and make you famous with those 18 other cats just like ya. Yeah, we know: You don't really need the press.

That's why we want ya.

en hopup veritas

THE MORRISON

By Hop Up Staff - Photos by Rick Amado

Absolute hot rod history. One of the coolest hot rod roadsters of the early 50s, a Hop Up feature car...restored to perfection. "Magnificent" is what owner/restorer Jack Stirnemann heard all weekend at Pebble Beach.

You can see in Amado's photos that the word was well chosen by the dozens of blue bloods and others who uttered it.

Jack brought the car to Hop Up for a photo session before Pebble Beach, before the others, deferring to the car's original publisher and the soul that is Hop Up. Know well, boys, that the soul of this car belongs in Hop Up.

Jack bought the car from the late Ermie Immerso in the mid-nineties. He knew Ermie had a number of roadsters that he was not selling, but made the call anyhow, and Ermie said, "I'll sell one, if you'll pay my price. Sure." He'd had the car since 1980. Jack called his Pal Don Thelen (yeah, Buffalo) and asked him to preview the car. Don did, and soon Jack and Cathy were on their way to The Golden State with the car trailer. The only clue to the deuce's provenance was a comment Ermie made: "If you want to know

STIRNEMANN '32

anything about the car, I know the guy in Phoenix who usta own it."

Some time later, while at the SEMA show, Ermie ran across Stirnemann and said, "Here, I wrote down the name and number of the guy in Phoenix." Jack didn't call immediately, but eventually did. Gary Godbehere was sure enough a past owner/caretaker of the car, and he was able to tell the tale of an outstanding Hop Up feature car from 1951. One great bit of info was that the car had appeared in "Best Hot Rods", a Fawcett

publication in 1953. Hairpin mounts, for example, were undeniably the ones still with the car, and another link was made back to Hop Up. And Walker Morrison. Now we have a story. Proof of the hot rod's appearance in mags of the day. And first-hand recollections of how it was...back then. Ahhhhhh!

Morrison was a Burbank guy (we got friends there), and a lady friend late in life was a female 200 MPH Club member. She, Ralph McFarland – a friend of Morrison – and others were interviewed. Diligent research, done because he cared about chronicling the correct history of the rod, resulted in a perfect and complete chronology of

the car's life since it was stock...and a file of documentation that suggests Jack is even more of an anthropologist than the consummate car builder he is.

After the Hop Up photo session they took the car to the Pebble Beach Concours. Won second place. Yup. Some of us have a different take on the win, the place and show of the deal but... See for yourself.

The highlight of that long weekend for the relieved restorer was the road tour that is optional for entrants. The gorgeous roadster was not outclassed by bigger, richer and more notorious company; rather, it held it's own in performance and appearance, and panache. That's one for the home team, Boys!

From there they went to Pleasanton for the "Goodguise" event and that huge crowd made our Builders happier yet that they had gone to the trouble. Done the right thing.

Swarmed with attention and back pats, the ride to St. Louis was a good one.

We think that wry grin on Jack Stirnemann's face might just be there...for keeps.

Pages 8/9: This is an example of the pinnacle of 50s hot rod aesthetics. Posture, appointments, finish rate this car with the most notable highboys of the day, that day or any day; the Stirnemann Brothers restoration, supported by research, interviews and advanced hot rod forensics, is second to none. Yes, we said none!

Pages 10/11: Collage of Amado photography won't require words. Know what I mean? Yup. They'd be in the way.

Top: The rig has a smart look goin' away, too, of course. It drove away from Pebble Beach with a second place.

Above: Filled, dropped axle is genuine, old piece that is sprung from a Model A front crossmember. Frame showed remnants of a Hemi installed in 50s then SBC in 60s. Owner Stirnemann made all repairs and brought chassis to this exceptional state.

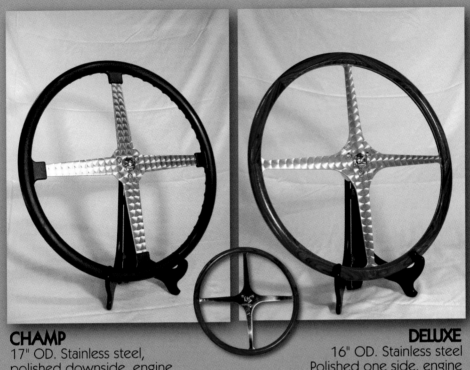

A Fine Whine

There's just something about the whine of a quick-change rearend that sends a chill up the spine of any true hot rodder. I remember the first time I was first assaulted by early Halibrands well over decade ago while following a group of cars as they wound a path up the San Bernardino Mountains in Southern California during the River City Reliability Run. Tagging along in a rental car wasn't my exact idea of fun, but it got me as close as possible to these killer gow-jobs as they built their revs higher with each and every gear change. Somehow things transform as time goes by, but they also stays the same. While heading out to shoot Howard Hastings' bitchin' Model A roadster I was again following, this time while lugging along photo equipment, as his drop-top slowly transversed cobbled old town roads in Barre, Massachusetts on the way to our shoot. As

soon as a clean stretch of asphalt opened up though, Howard gave his hot flathead a stab and made it shoot up the road like a load of buckshot, all the while its quick change was whining like a call of glory. That said, Howard's journey with his roadster reads like an encyclopedia of dedication to the hobby, with his influence for the build dating back to his teens.

Growing up in Orange, MA in the 50s Howard had the benefit of living in the same town as the famed Orange Drags, where on the third Sunday of every month, some of the most wicked hot rods and drag cars in the East would stop in to make runs on the famed strip. At the age of ten, Howard would ride his bike to the strip and stare in awe as these fire-breathing warriors would shake the fillings out of your teeth. While growing up, he always made it to the track without

By Chuck Vranas

fail, and by the time he was attending art school his friends in the Carbs Hot Rod Club invited him into the inner sanctum by having him letter all the cars scheduled to race, as they did the tech inspections. It was this first hands-on opportunity to get up close and personal with the cars that Howard knew he had a calling with, which would follow him as he aged. As time passed, Howard recalls being at Hershey decades later, and while walking the swap meet he came across a set of vintage Edmunds heads and a three-pot intake that grabbed his attention; enough to bring all his youthful memories full-circle. Always having a fascination with early flatheads since hearing them roar down the strip at Orange, he bought up the parts, and by the time he arrived back home had sorted out a plan to build the roadster of his dreams. Howard often recalled one of the most influential cars

of his youth being a superb chopped and channeled Deuce roadster owned by good friend Roger Bergquist, who he had not seen in ages. The spark of preparing to build his own car lit a fuse that led him back to visit with Roger, actually bringing the two friends back together. While catching up, Howard inquired into what ever happened to the roadster that he so fondly recalled, when he was led into the back of the shop where it sat, having been asleep for the last 30 years. Not

Above: From the front angle you can easily appreciate all of the personality in Howard's roadster. The combination of just enough dark purple vibe on the body melds well with the black Deuce chassis while the weathered yellow Kelsey-Hayes wires close the deal. Neat touches like the custom-fabbed windshield, split bones, and cycle fenders add tons of character.

Thanks to a set of carefully selected big & littles and the right suspension, Howard's roadster has a perfect stance. There's nothing like a Halibrand V8 center peeking out from the back, especially when combined with a set of '48 Ford taillights, and a racer-styled gas fill on the back deck.

only would Howard get loads of tips on the build of his new roadster, he also inspired Roger to unearth his car and get it back on the road. Man, this is what it's all about!

Howard wanted his roadster to embody as many original parts as possible, so he located a clean Deuce chassis and started gathering parts that were loaded with just enough little-book cool to keep the car period perfect. To get the proportions just right for the Model A roadster body, the rails were pinched at the cowl and Model A front and rear crossmembers were added to the mix. Up front a vintage dropped axle was matched up with an un-split Deuce wishbone combined with a matching spring, tube shocks, and '40 Ford brakes for stopping power. Nothing sez hot rod like a Halibrand quick-change rear, so Howard matched up an early V8 center section with '37 Ford axles, while suspension chores are handled by a Model A rear spring and Houdaille shocks, while '40 Ford brakes round everything out. Kelsey-Hayes 16-inch wires with wide whites bring the roadsters stance to perfection like nothing else could. For plenty of power, Howard started with a '48 Ford block opened up to 265ci and then assembled it with a 4" Merc crank, Isky 77-B stick, Edmunds heads, and a Tattersfield 2-pot intake breathing deep through a pair of 97-series Stromberg carbs, while a '39 Ford box selects the gears. Finding a suitable roadster body proved quite difficult while living on the East Coast's rustbelt, so Howard placed a call to Brookville for one of their killer '29 roadster bodies. He then got busy designing a one-off windshield for the

Top: Howard built the flathead in the roadster using a vintage speed shop full of go-fast parts like Edmunds finned aluminum heads, Fenton headers, Tattersfield 2-pot, and Stromberg 97-series carbs. Filled with an Isky stick and a 4-inch Merc crank, the engine has more than enough power to hold its own on the highway while scaring the livestock around town.

Center and Left: There's nothing like getting comfy sitting in your favorite easy chair! Howard was able to make great use of the leather from an old 50s recliner to help create the interior for the roadster while adding a custom made dash top made from birds-eye maple. Monitoring the car's vitals comes thanks to an array of original Stewart Warner gauges while a vintage banjo wheel of unknown lineage navigates the turns.

car that echoed the art-deco era of the early Auburn speedsters. Starting first in pine, he then looked to Roger for help, as he's a pattern maker, to dial it all in before it was finally cast in bronze. The completed piece gave the car an instant calling card like no other. More personal touches continued with custom fabbed rear aluminum fenders matched up with painted units up front fashioned from '35 Ford spare tire covers and a hood top loaded with louvers by Roy Idman.

Settling into the interior of the car is a comfortable as sitting on an old leather easy chair, since that's exactly where the hides came from. Howard topped the dash with birds-eye maple and filled it with a bevy of original Stewart Warner gauges to keep track of all the vital signs. Future plans for the roadster include incorporating an early Riley grille into a track-style nose, the addition of a set of E&J headlights, and the fabrication of a removable steel top. Howard tells us that the greatest thing about the car is that it's a work in progress that he is able to enjoy on a daily basis, especially when he hits the road with good friends Roger Bergquist and Russ Daley. We think Howard said it best regarding his car: "The roadster is an ongoing endeavor, sort of a sculpture being enjoyed while it's unfinished. It's an old car that drives like one with three speeds, vintage suspension, noisy quick-change, comfortable seats, and beautiful gauges to look at. I prefer driving it to washing it and don't expect to ever finish it." We said, we couldn't agree more!

Tim Thompson's
HOP UP CAR

Tim Thompson owns the 'Low Lucky' '32 Roadster, a car we admired for many years, but had no real knowledge of the owner.

When a letter came in from Illinois asking if we'd approve the use of the Hop Up logo style hand-painted on to an old bomber jacket, we said, "yeah, sure;" Then came the pictures of the finished product with a nice model and all. Hell, this cat does it right. Still didn't know he owned Low Lucky.

Well, a season or two went by and Tim called. "Yeah, I did the jacket, but now I'm gonna do a 3W and I want to paint the Hop Up Logo on the cowl." Kind of a nose-art Hop Up tribute. Well, we are beginning to see that Tim Thomson identifies with the Hop Up ethic. Style. He gets it. Must be one of the eighteen other guys, beside you.

"Well, yeah. Is it gonna be a pretty bone car?" we risked. "Yeah." Okay, we're in.

Below: We didn't have to go far to find a slick site to shoot the car: Tim Thompson is a custom home builder and he built this one for himself.

The year the car came out, it started life at the San Fran' R 'n C show...then at the GNRS (the Daddy...yeah, "Oakland"...we know.) in Pomona!...then Cobo Hall, and the Chi World of Wheels. Pretty damned auspicious. They even stopped on the way out to Cali and unloaded the car at Bonneville (we been there, we tell ya?) and ran it and photo'd it. They claim to be the first members of the "20 MPH Club." It is about the fun of hot rods after all, ain't it, Boys?

At one of those show swindles, Carbon, Utah custom maniac Bo Huff approached Tim and said, "You own this?" Now, ya gotta know, Bo has an...aura...about him... Tim says, "(gulp) Yes, yes I do." kind of apologetically.

"That's a tidy little car."

Better 'n a trophy. Bet ya Tim won't forget that one.

(We had an almost identical incident with Mr. Huff in the pits in Bonneville in 1990. He liked our deuce tudor and made an out of the way sweep through the pits to drive over, get out and offer his compliment. Very much like the one he shared with Tim. Huff's an intimidating, legendary, talented and easy-with-a-compliment guy. Cool. Ed)

Next, the coup de grace is a major feature in TRJ (doesn't leave much for us, do it??!) Tim has begun to complete the plan and drive the car. Fits and spurts at first, but finally in to the permanent rotation with the

roadster and whatever else comes down the pike. Ya think he can do a third spectacular car? A trifecta?

Oh yeah, buddy. Oh, yeah.

Top: Balanced '58 Cad mill is scraped and armed to 414 c.i. All parts are pre- '58, including Edelbrock 3x2 manifold, solid Isky cam, etc.
Below: '40 Ford wheel is on a truck column. '58 SW gauges are consistent with pre-'58 rule, including that Harley Speed Tracker Speedo.
Bottom: External plating is all nickel (nice touch, lots of work!); stock, uncut body lost cowl lights, bumpers, splash pan. Coupe is featured in Hop Up road shows that Tim puts on throughout the Midwest, led by the World of Wheels Show in Chi.

The
MAX GILMORE ROADSTER

By Hop Up Staff - Photos by Rick Amado

Jack up the radiator cap and...yeah, you've done it, too, huh? You know the core is a good one and you also know that some portion of the price you pay will be for naught. Worthless. Chuck it. According to plan, you strip it down to what's usable and add parts you've accumulated with this very car in mind. It's part of the deal and it's what ya signed up for.

The car had been visible for a long time, so he knew its credentials, e.g. he knew what would be good for the roadster project and what would go to the swap meet. It was a real '32 frame and it was a real '29 roadster body, but they had been the foundation of something too street-roddish for Max Gilmore. He blew it apart according to his vision, and made it this trad roadster, pleasing to the eye, timeless in style, and a permanent addition to his stable.

We first saw the hot rod on a Reliability Run and were impressed by how different it was from other "Black '29 on deuce rails" cars we've seen. It's cool that you can take

a base formula for a good car and innovate, personalize it with your own combination of trad treatments, and, it becomes an individual. You know, make your own best call on frame choice; ride height; spring combo, number of leaves, eyes reversed or no; shock choice and location; axle dropped or not, if so, how much? Plated or not? Engine, performance options, trans, rear, open/closed driveline; brakes, wheels, width, diameter, color; body mods, paint or prime, more color ideas to bang around in your maxed-out brain; stock

shield or chopped? How much? Interior. A million instrument cluster ideas. Steering wheel, column, column drop. Switches.

Ya don't get that with a restoration.

Building a hot rod is a personal expression of your own best call *at that time*. Since they are never done, they say, you can revise, change, switch, modify as you go...as though it's some kinda ferric cell division, inevitable

Above: Stroker McGurk would be proud. Magoo. And Pollard. As we say, there are base rules and the combination of 'approved' treatments is up to the guy with the vision. Max got 'em all in there. Just another black roadster? Naw.

and heading toward perfect adaptation to its environment and circumstance.

That's why we *screw them up* instead of restore them. They become our own. This is the Max Gilmore roadster. Always will be. In a hundred years the name might be hyphenated but the first name will be *Gilmore.*

Above: We like Lincoln wheels, Auburn dashes and cut tops: all the tricks guys used to make a Ford look/feel like a big ol' Lincoln or Packard or Duesenberg. Blacked-out hardware lends an austere, all business vibe that – again – personalizes the car.

Below: Sunset image romanticizes the little Ford, suggests all kinds of possibilities after the sun drops past the hill, no?

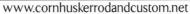

A Turtle Deck T...
Based on Traditional Styling and Built with Sound Engineering

PHOENIX T

By Jon Gobetti

Dutch Eshelman is no stranger to the pages of Hop Up. He spent a lifetime building dozens of traditional hot rods similar to Grabowski's and Ivo's Ts. He would complete and debut each hand-crafted rod, more often than not, at the Nats in Louisville. Every year a discerning rodder would covet Dutch's traditional ride, and Dutch would return to Iowa with a pocketful of green to build another. Two recent examples can be found in Hop Up Special No. 2, page 14. Since moving to Arizona, Dutch has plied his craft as a body man and mechanic at some of the best rod shops in the Valley of the Sun. Now he just builds cars for himself and a few close friends in a compact two-story workshop behind his home in east Mesa. Every new project is an artistic creation, built using common sense engineering, traditional building techniques, eye-pleasing proportions and a perfect stance.

This T-bucket, as well the last to grace these pages, were built from bits and pieces collected over a lifetime of scrounging metal frames, old bodies, and period-perfect mechanicals. This one's got two doors, no fenders, no roof, no ugly paint, no cartoon characteristics and no bullshit geegaws or doodads.

The foundation, a 1929 Chrysler frame, with so many handmade modifications they can't all be listed here, is a 109" wheelbase providing excellent handling characteristics. Up front, a '37 Ford Tube axle with a Model A modified spring softens the ride, while '32 Ford radius rods square everything to the frame. A Ford F-1 steering box directs the Motorwheel 16 x 4 wire rims shod with Firestone ribbed 500-16 implementation tires. A pair of Fomoco '46 backing plates with '40 drums front and rear activated by an F-1 master cylinder pull brake duty.

To the rear, a Halibrand quick-change (Q.C.) uses 4:11 ring and pinion to turn and burn those 750-16 knobby Firestones. This is all supported by transverse springs dampened by friction shocks. One unique feature: the front of each rear leaf spring perch is incorporated into, and supports, the side nerf bars.

Power comes from a '55 Chevy 265; a .125 overbore brings the total cubic inches to 283. It's dressed with Corvette script, staggered hole, valve covers. O_2 and unleaded gas mix in four two-barrel Strombergs, then flows through a Wieand four-pot manifold. A Grant dual-coil Flamethrower ignition system sparks the mixture in the cylinder heads. A 098 bump stick (the hottest factory cam in '55) activates the solid lifters sending spent gases from the block through a set of Headman headers with modified down tubes and collectors. A '39 Lincoln trans filled with 25 tooth Zephyr gears and transfers torque through the driveshaft to the aforementioned Q.C.

Dutch massaged the '25 T bucket's body until it was perfectly smooth, and then coated all the surfaces in gray primer. Using only the lower half of the original windshield, Dutch removed 4" from its height. After filling the stock dash, he installed an original set of curved glass, Stewart Warner gauges. A Model A steering wheel tops the home-built column. Under the turtle deck's lid, an owner-built tank holds 14 gallons of gas. The grill shell, also a '25, splits a pair of Corte headlights. A single Owl taillight mounts to the driver-side of the turtle deck's rear pan. If, for some obscure reason, the starter should ever fail, a clever, hand-fabricated, push bar can be pressed into action.

The single interior creature comfort is the seat: a commercial, brown, bus-line vinyl stitched up by Brian Cline, the upholsterer, and Dutch.

This is not a radical, blown mega-cubic-inch, in-your-face, cartoon T-bucket, but rather a refined, well proportioned, old style hot rod that's pleasing to the eye, easy on the pocket book, and a delight to drive, easily meeting the benchmark set by Grabowski and Ivo.

Clockwise from top left: The front of each rear leaf spring perch is incorporated into, and supports, the side nerf bars. Note the stock upward curve of the '29 Chrysler frame eliminates the need for Z-ing the frame. • Connecting the front friction shocks to the split deuce radius rods not only softens the ride, it keeps the front end clean and uncluttered. Notice the use of a stock generator rather than an alternator in keeping with the overall traditional theme of the hot rod. • The spartan interior's single creature comfort is the seat covered in commercial brown bus-line vinyl. • Power comes from a '55 Chevy 265 punched out to 283 cubic inches. Induction: a staggered Wieand four-pot manifold fed by four two barrel Strombergs.

Below: Tucked beneath the turtle deck, a Halibrand quick-change running 4:11s turns those 750:16 knobby Firestones. Neat push bar. eh?

EVOLUTION

By Chuck Vranas

Looking like something out of a time-warp from the 40s at either El Mirage or Bonneville, Pete's coupe brings just enough style mixed with subtleties to keep it timeless. The bull nose, combined with a full hood, perfect chop, and low-slung E&Js, makes its presence one that any true diehard enthusiast could study for hours.

Nestled way up in the woods and off the beaten path in Northboro, Massachusetts is a small workshop where the term gow-job has thrived for close to a decade. Unless you know exactly where it is, you can forget about finding it. Walking into Pete Flaven's reclusive shop is like stepping back in time. The walls and ceilings are filled with vintage parts...some thanks to miserably early walks through rain soaked swap meets, others long left for dead at what used to resemble local salvage yards. In one corner, a greasy Caddy engine lays waiting for its next home, while a freshly swept pile of metal shavings gives you an indication that this is one place where heavy duty cutting and welding shows creativity is hard at work. As the years have passed, Flaven's style has become well known, and it's easy to track his own personal evolution as a builder from where he first started.

Heavily influenced by hot rods of the 40s and early 50s, Pete is one of the forefathers of the East Coast Hardcore scene and a founding member of the legendary Alter Boys car club. He brought the coast's roots to the forefront years ago when he first dropped the bomb with a purely wicked, no-nonsense '30 Chevy coupe that reeked evil, thanks to its

stance, edgy 4-pot fed Nailhead, and '39 Ford truck grille...all built on a budget of less than three grand. Soldiering on past the coupe, he focused on a few intermediate projects, each with unique personalities, including a six-banger urged modified that finally led him to the project lying on these pages. The more things change, the more they stay the same... Heavy words that outline the dynamics of one person's vision to stay true to his roots while growing as a builder. For this project, Pete was faced with a number of challenges in building his '33 coupe. The car would need to evoke a 40s-esque style that would have looked equally at home whether it was at time trials at El Mirage, waiting to get staged at Orange Drag Strip, or cruising the local streets.

Everyone who lives back East knows that finding vintage steel in decent shape is a bitch, thanks to vicious winters that have no mercy on metallurgical composition. This, of course, makes getting started quite a challenge in finding suitable donor parts. Pete started the project with a gennie spine that rolled off Henry's assembly line some 74 years ago. After being cleaned up, it was fully boxed, given a hard 5-inch kick out back, and filled

with stock front and rear cross-members. The front suspension evolved from a combination of a 4-inch dropped axle supported by a pair of split bones that previously saw duty on an old stock car, while a stock '33 spring with a reversed eye main leaf and Columbus velvet-ride front shocks with custom mounts help soften the ride. Out back, it's all business with a '55 Chevy rear suspended by custom fabbed triangulated radius rods, while a pair of NOS GM-Delco hydraulic tube shocks and a stock rear spring (with a few leaves removed) keep it all planted to the ground. Set to roll on a quartet of original '40 Ford 16x4 steelies up front with 16x5's out back, only Firestone wide whites could bring the final dazzle into the mix.

With the base of the coupe heading in the right direction, it was time to focus on the coupe's body and all of the help it would need to breathe life back into it. For this part of the build, Pete called on good friend Donnie Smart of Smart's Hot Rod and Custom of Valdese, North Carolina for both his expertise and his bitchin' sheet metal parts to help resurrect the weathered coupe's body. Donnie also supplied the much needed critical dimensions that would dictate the coupe's panel placement and fitment. Pete then fabricated an adjustable inner body jig

that allowed him to pre-adjust the cowl to the B-pillars to then make other adjustments as needed. Once the truckload of new sheet metal arrived, including complete floors, 3 window door top conversions, sail panels, upper deck lid panel, rear quarter panels, and tail corners, Pete got busy and didn't quit till the coupe was released from life-support! With everything now rock solid, Pete hammered the lid 4 inches, leaned the A-pillars back 8 degrees and gave it a subtle 2 1/2-inch channel to give the coupe just the right attitude adjustment. Pete's personal style is something that we've come to expect on every hop-up he builds, and for the coupe he designed a one-off "bull-nose" to give it a calling card that hasn't been seen on the scene in quite a long time. Working with Russ Daly of Cumberland, Rhode Island, he had Russ fabricate both the hood top and sides that would bring everything together perfectly, sending a chill up the spine of every diehard traditionalist who has seen the car since. Capping off the front end with a set of gennie E&J headlights mounted dramatically low on custom mounts, the car's soul started to emerge.

Nothing sez stoke like a '55 Olds 324-inch mill filled with a hot stick and topped with a once-polished Edmunds 2-pot sucking heavily through a pair of 97s. Pete rebuilt the engine and peppered it with vintage parts, including a polished Cragar bellhousing and Wilcap starter crossover that was linked to a '67 Ford 4-speed top-loader and classic Hurst shifter topped with a custom swan neck. With everything coming together, Pete handed the bodywork and paint duties over to Eli English of Pittsfield, New Hampshire to give the coupe a razor-sharp body and lay down a subtle coating of custom-blended gloss. Emerging from the spray-booth with its newfound glamour, Pete focused on the interior, which would stay era-correct while infusing just enough personality to separate it from the rest. Using an original '33 Ford dash, he added his own custom engine-turned instrument and glove box covers, filled the holes with vintage military-issue Stewart Warner gauges, while a seductive swan-necked Waltham 8-day clock plucked from an old Auburn lets him know when it's time to head home. Topping an original '33 ford seat with classic fabric keeps the interior comfortable while he navigates through an original '40 Ford steering wheel linked to a '48 Ford F-1 steering box. Plans are for the coupe to officially hit the road with a trip to Bonneville for the 60th Anniversary, where we know the mixture of salt & style will have this coupe looking just plain wicked! As with any undertaking us this magnitude, Pete would like to send thanks out to all of the great friends who helped make it possible, including Donnie Smart, Eli English, Jim Gove and Paul Aldrich.

Top: Period perfect and ready for action, the 324-inch Olds bent-eight looks right at home nailed to the rails of Pete's coupe. Adorned with a smattering of vintage chrome and a weathered old polished Edmunds intake it's a mill that's all business. It comes to life with the touch of the starter, breathing heavy through the Strombergs and exhaling with plenty of ruckus through straight pipes out back.

Center: Timeless. . . the combination of plaid seat fabric covering the original seat base and rubber floor matting, blended with subtle touches like a homespun swan neck shifter topped with a unique vintage shift knob gives the interior a real welcome feeling. Stewart Warner military-issue gauges, a Waltham 8-day clock on its original mount, and '40 Ford wheel give the coupe a level of distinctiveness that is unparalleled.

Right: Hunkered down and ready for any challengers to make a move, the coupe gets loads of style points, thanks to a perfect stance, mirror-straight body lines, cool '50 Pontiac tail lights, and neat aluminum deck lid bolted into place and held secure by a pair of unknown vintage deck hinges.

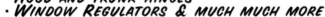

A DAY ON THE SALT

By Peter Vincent

As with many hot rod photo sessions, especially at Bonneville and out on the great expanse of the salt, what starts out as a very controlled shoot evolves somewhat naturally into one that isn't. This drives some people nuts, but I have learned to allow the evening to take its own direction, and in doing that, it usually evolves into an interesting adventure, and everyone has a good time. Of course, it doesn't always work out that way, but this one did, I think. The shoot was originally going to involve three cars, all still in their very original patina'd original paint and body. Each had a personality of its own, and each was driven out to the salt from some distance. The only "kind-of" problem was that not all cars were there at the same time, so, in the one major group photo, one was missing as he had to leave early, but, he was there for the original set up, and it was a car I definitely wanted included. It was Jim Johnson's 1940 Ford Coupe deluxe.

It was Jim's '40 coupe that started this story. The first time I noticed it was in 2005, when he had the car parked out in front of the casino in Wendover, Nevada with no hood showing a three deuce'd small block, beautiful original desert patina'd paint, a dropped front end, original torque thrust and pie cut cheater slicks. The interior was still in the original tan mohair... This car looked like it had just crawled out of the bright and dry desert sun, and was, in fact, found in a small New Mexico town in 1986. Jim is the third owner of the car, and he says it has never been in a garage, at least for the past 20 years. Jim's son runs the Hot Rod Haven Shop in Albuquerque, which is where some of the updates and conversion took place. Under the night lights of the casino, it flat

stood out and truly looked unique. I actually left a note on his windshield asking whether or not he was interested in selling the car. It was one of those images I couldn't get out of my head. It was even the right color (cloud mist gray), at least for me. The damned coupe was parked perfectly under the lights, and it sat right (with a 4-inch dropped axle in front and TCI parallels in the rear). I ran into Jim during the next few days out on the salt, and he let me take it for a spin. I took it up to about 70 mph just outside of the pit area towards the mountains and found that it drove beautifully, tracked fine, and didn't wander in the least.

David Lyon's '40 Delivery was a push car at Bonneville in 1962 for Vic Colvin's hemi powered record holding roadster. Other than the Mordrop front axle and the F100 brakes, the car is stock, and yeah, that's the original paint on it and the original interior. It sat in a barn for 40 years until being "found" in 2005. This is one of "those" cars that you hear about every once in a while. It still has some original Bonneville stickers on the cowl. I did not realize how "nice" this car was until I started photographing the interior, particularily the rear area. The cargo area, or the wood floor above the spare tire compartment, was in great condition. This Delivery was, or I should say is, a great find in all of its original authentic beauty. The more I look at the images, the more I like it.

Mike Abssy's (of Schraders Speed & Style) '36 is sitting on a '38 chassis with a 4-inch dropped axle, reverse-eyed spring with parallel leafs and a Currie 9-inch in the rear. Whats is a bit different is the '73 472-inch Caddy engine hooked to a '99 Camaro 6-speed tranny. Mike said the car was originally grey and it was painted black with a brush or mitten long ago...the rest is mother nature's rendering. He did not touch the outside.

The real sidestep on the original story was two phaetons out of the Cincinnati, Ohio area that kept attracting my attention. When you are at Bonneville, you see a lot of cars, many that you would like to photograph. The problem is, that unless you set up some time schedule to meet, because of the amount of geographical area that everything is spread out, you might never see them again. Well, the only night that this would work with these guys was the same night that I had set up with the other cars. On top of that, Mike Whitney showed up with this ultra chopped

Previous page: Profile of Jim Johnson's desert fresh (slightly refreshed) '40 coupe out on the salt of Bonneville in 2005 sans hood and one headlight ring.

Far left: This is how I first saw Jim's '40 coupe under the lights of the Nugget Casino in Wendover, Nevada. Damn thing stood out like a beacon of light for me. I left a note on his windshield.

Top: David Lyon's "Grocery Wagon" had "been to Bonneville before" (notice the early Bonneville stickers on the cowl) as a push car, an unbelievable garage find. What else can I say, except I wish I had been the one who found it.

Bottom left: An interior shot of David's Sedan Delivery, as found. The back area was just as nice.

Bottom right: An engine view of Jim Johnson's 1940 Coupe Deluxe showing a pretty classic setup with early finned valve covers and a 3-deuce carb setup. Jim kept the original wiring in place to keep the look.

(10-inches) 3-window Plymouth coupe with a track nose that had to be part of the session, especially since he was also out of Ohio area and knew Matt and Shawn. He had Joshua Shaw with him, whom I had met a few years earlier at Bonneville with his chopped '32 Tudor. Anyway, the "Cincinnati Kids" were in Matt & Ken Reynolds' '32 Ford Phaeton, the #4 car. This car was found in a Kentucky junkyard, where it had been residing since 1984, after being in a garage fire. The car was a full-fendered showcar at one time. Matt drove the car to Bonneville in 2005 and 2006. This year he drove to the L.A. Roadster show on Father's Day for another cross-country trip. Next year he says it will be Bonneville again. The tub is sitting on a stock '32 frame with a 350 Chev and a '67 Mustang rear end. The steering is a '59 Corvette setup. The wheels are '40 Ford steelies shod with Firestone tires. The car is full of visual details, like the Buick portholes in the hood sides. Shawn Burden's flat black

'29 Ford Phaeton is running a Chevy 327 and a Frankland quickchange rear end. ET3 16-inch wheels set up the rear and skinny Halibrands on the front. The car is covered with lots of louvers both front and back.

As I previously mentioned, just as we were starting to setup, another car from Ohio drove up with Mike Whitney sitting in the driver's seat of his severely chopped 1932 3-window Plymouth Coupe, and Joshua Shaw as a passenger. The Plymouth has been chopped 10-inches with the front pillars leaned to the back and a '32 Dodge truck windshield relieved 2-inches up into the roof for visibility. The nose, hood and grille are all hand-made by the owner. The car is running a 331 Caddy with 2x2 Edmunds manifold and a couple of 97s with SP tops. The car is also running a very rare Paul Kollstedt quick-change rear end, which is one of the three still known to exist in the country. These were actually made in Paul's home from the late 40s through the early 80s. The car is named

the "Richcraft Special" after the Richcraft Speedshop that was owned by a friend of Mike's Dad in Ohio in the early 50s. The rear wheels are Pop Dryer's, and the interior is very spartan with a narrowed bomber seat, an original cast Richcraft gas pedal and a Bell steering wheel. The deck and hood sides are filled with louvers, and the cowl steering is a home-made Saginaw setup.

It was a great evening with great light.

Opposite page: A late evening shot of two "almost original paint" cars shot in 2006 at Bonneville. Note the added hood and headlight door on Jim Johnson's '40 coupe. Mike Abssy's '36 3-window adds to the perfect pair. Mike's '36 was painted black over the original gray with either a brush or a mitten some time in the past.

Right: Mike Abssy's '36 is running a 472 c.i.d. Caddy into a '99 Camaro 6-speed tranny on back to a Currie 9-inch rear.

Below: Two tubs out of Philly. Matt & Ken Reynolds' purple '32 (#4) and Shawn Burden's nasty, very much louvered flat black '29 Ford Phaeton both made the trip all the way out to Bonneville.

Top left: A zebra striped interior shot of Matt and Ken Reynolds' '32 Phaeton. Note the gauge setup and Bell wheel.

Center: A rear end shot of Shawn Burden's '29 Phaeton showing all of the louvers and a Franklin Q.C.

Top Right: Another detail of Shawn's '29 showing the Buick drums, chromed and drilled backing plates, and that great blue light.

Below: A front view of Shawn's '29 showing the front louver treatment, how it sits, the light treatment, and the skinny fronts and big rears all mounted on unpolished Halibrands. Perfect...

Another car that I photographed in 2006 that kind-of fits in with the overall story is Tom Christian's '33 Ford Pickup monikered with a "Moonlight Speed Shop" painting on the doors. It seems that Tom (at a very young age in Carson City, Nevada) "lifted" some old wheels from a garage and got caught. Well, the police called it the "moonlight auto supply" and the moonlight part stuck with Tom for the rest of his life. He also learned his lesson. The '33 is powered by a 350 horse 327 with 3-deuces and Corvette valve covers followed by a very streetable T5 tranny and a Ford 9-inch rear. The car is on the ground thanks to a Z'd frame, a 6-inch dropped tube axle, a body that is chopped 6-inches and the fact that it is channeled 6-inches over the frame. The '33 grille has been sectioned 3.5-inches. The wheels are from a Nash. The lettering and striping were applied by Dale Weber out of Reno, Nevada, and Mother Nature added a natural desert rust finish to the rest of the car. The "bomber" seats are comfortable, and the detail work is interesting and well put together.

Above: Tom Christian's '33 Ford Pickup running a 350 horse 327. Note some of the interesting detail work, such as the radiator cover, the lower grille skid and the headlights. This car was full of great details.

Below: Christian's "MoonLight Speed Shop" '33 out on the salt of Bonneville in 2006 in original desert patina. The wheels are Nash born.

The only car missing from this shot was Jim Johnson's '40 Coupe. He had to leave early. The "new" addition to the group is Mike Whitney's 1932 Plymouth 3-window Coupe, the "Richcraft Special," which showed up at the last minute that evening with Joshua Shaw in the passenger seat. Perfect addition. Could not leave it out. This is an example of the great variety of vehicles that show up "out" on the salt of Bonneville. Thanks guys.

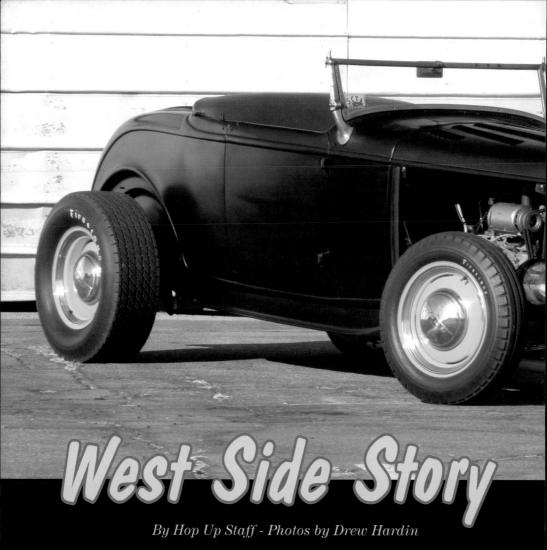

West Side Story

By Hop Up Staff - Photos by Drew Hardin

Dick Wade is a 'West Side' guy (west side of L.A., that is). The traditional hot rod culture there is typical, but unique in some ways in that much of Los Angeles talent was on that side of City Hall. Bud Hand, Wes Cooper, Norm Grant, Ed Donovan and more, including the younger Dick Wade.

The story? What separates the interesting cars from the pedestrian is...the story.

A guy named Harry Ringer built his deuce roadster in '46-'47 almost like Bob McGee's famous roadster. They were buddies, and the cars were even called twins. The fraternal part comes in when you note that Ringer had less money to spend on his car than McGee, so there were several differences .

One time, Wade had an opportunity to buy the Ringer car, but it got away, so, lest we mislead you, this ain't that car.

Dick found this car at the LA Roadsters Father's Day swap meet in about '74, and it consisted of a body, frame, front and rear suspension members and about half a barn full of parts, including N.O.S. (yes) Kinmonts, an N.O.S. Halibrand Quickchange rear end and more. Sounds like enough to us, right?

Parts accumulation began in a slow but earnest way, and, during that 7 to 8 year spell, Dick got just about everything else he needed from...discarded parts from the Harry Ringer car! Yep. Some lunk made

Left: Wade roadster benefits from lots of NOS parts like Kinmonts, quick change, tires and more.

Above: Stanchions and windshield frame have that "old time religion." Faux patina has become trite, these days, but this hot iron is all genuine, not faked, and was this way long before the present trend.

Below: '48 Merc 259.4" steel crankshaft was de-stroked to 3 5/8". bore is 3 3/8". S.C.o.T. blower and an Isky cam came from Osan Yumori's blown dry lakes coupe.

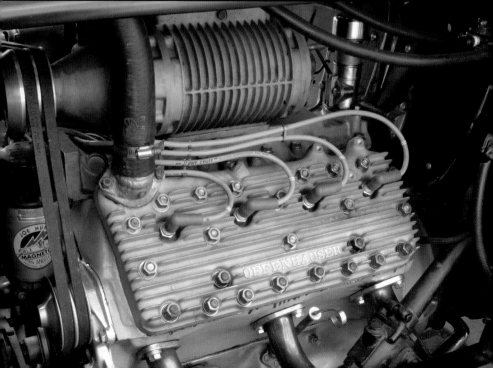

something else out of the car in that 70s frenzy to "Resto" and "Indy" old Fords into something they would only need to be for about one decade. Transitory. Temporary. Un-permanent.

Wade's plans for his roadster project were to go drag racing. The venue of choice was Orange County Raceway, and, after cannibalizing his 3w for parts...when he just about had the rod ready to go...they had the last race at OCR and...he missed it.

Oh, well, there would be plenty of years of street duty off and on, so it worked out OK.

But then the big 75th year of the Deuce inspired Dick to get both the roadster and the three window up and running again, including taking the roadster to the Antique Nationals Drags which long ago had found a new home at LA County Raceway in Palmdale. The old roadster came out, got some fixin' done, only to find it had an engine with great parts but a bad block, and so it missed the drags again. Oh: This was the last race at LACR!!! Seems to be a trend here, eh? Let's hope that the next iteration of change for this real hot rod survivor doesn't spell the end of another drag strip!!!

So, the car is back into driving rotation with Wade's other stuff which, as a matter of fact, includes a similarly pure and correct '32 three window, which you'll see here next time out.

Hop Up Honor. Stay Honor

Top two: Car has a little wedge goin' for it; stance affords a good look at the quick change rear end with those Kinmonts on each end of it. **Center:** All business inside, '47 SW instrument panel, windshield and stanchions were off the Harry Ringer car. Shifter has a Muncie M 21 close ratio box on the bottom of it. **Bottom left:** NOS Kinmont Safe-Stop Disc Brakes and tires were NOS; 5" Bell axle and reversed spring eyes get 'er done in the lowering department.

Below: NOS Halibrand Culver City Q.C. has 11 gear sets to go with it; 'likes the 4.68 pair for drags. Kinmonts everywhere.

Charley O'Neal was a salesman at STICK CITY, a Hot Rod used car lot on Whittier Blvd. An old man came in one day in June 1974 and announced he had a 1932 Ford Hot Rod roadster for sale, $800 and not a penny less. Charley bought the roadster, cherry picked a few parts off of it and hauled it to the L.A. Roadster Show the following Sunday. He was asking $3000 and no takers. I bought the car the following Tuesday for $2800, top dollar at the time. That $2800 bought a nice body with doors, deck lid, dash, firewall, filled cowl vent & shell, hood, gas tank and a pair of junk front fenders and boards. The chassis consisted of a perfect pit-free frame with an A front cross member installed, '32 front end, '34 rear end, '40 backing plates & drums, and a '34 steering box. No engine or transmission. I started collecting parts in 1972 for a 1932 3-window coupe and with the Ringer parts, I was off to a good start. In 1975 I bought another roadster for parts.

I had the body dipped at L.A. Metal Stripping, primed it and stored it in my mother's garage. I took the frame to Pete Eastwood for cross member changes. Pete installed a Model A rear cross member to clear the quick-change and reinstalled the front properly. He modified the deuce pedal assembly for juice brakes & made motor mounts. He called and said the frame was done. When I arrived the frame looked perfect. Then Pete talked me into the Muncie 4 speed because he knew I liked to drag race. I left his shop, went straight to Offenhauser in Alhambra and inquired about an adaptor for mating a flathead Ford engine to Muncie transmission. They had one in stock, so it was back to Pete's shop with adaptor in hand. Pete had a big grin on his face when he saw the adaptor. Pete called a day later and said he didn't think there was enough of the original K member left for good support after cutting it up to clear the Muncie. That Muncie required a

pretty big hole. So Pete built a super strong K member to replace it.

Progress then began to slow. As the next Antique Nationals drew near, only the rear end was finished. I took drastic action and pulled the engine, firewall, and front end out of the 3 W coupe, installed them on the frame, dropped the body on, and with a little tinkering it was ready to race. At the next Antique Nationals it ran high 14s and mid 90s mph. Not bad for the fist time out.

I met some local Hot Rodders who were trying to start a local cruise night. and they prompted me to wire it up for street use. It took another two years to complete the front end, dash panel, paint and upholstery.

Meanwhile, the Antique National Drag Races were on again at L.A.C.R. in Palmdale. On a pass down the strip, an over-rev caused by a missed shift resulted in several broken tappets and a chewed up Webber F6 cam. Next year was much better. With the addition of an Isky 1017B Track cam and exhaust port dividers, the little blown De-stroker laid down its best run ever of 99.66 mph in 14.18 sec.

We didn't race for a couple of years. The next time out it blew a head gasket. I hadn't kept up with torque maintenance on aluminum heads, and there were some weak threads in some of the head stud holes. The car missed the next several years of racing because of my workload.

In 2002 I installed a 304ci engine out of an old dragster. It had everything: forged pistons, Isky 404 cam, huge valves, ported, polished, relieved and CRACKED. It only managed 96.44 in 14.70. That thing leaked all over, so I parked it. It collected dust until 2007.

The car was never really finished, as I kinda threw it together to race it at the "last" Nats. It's really ready for a redo, and the changes will include: a 304 c.i. Ardun, Pat Warren 2 speed V8 quick-change, and Okie Adams axle.

Customs

"Customs are for gettin' girls and hot rods are for gettin' rid of 'em."   *Robert Williams*

Even if he wasn't right, customs look like they might have the *savoir faire* to do the deed. They mighta been the tool a cat needed to demo his genteel side. Customs express the artistic eye of the craftsman: his desire to make the thing longer, lower, and look like something bigger, richer, and classier. It was to reflect the sensitivities of the owner to observers whose tastes and abilities may have been more pedestrian.

They pretty much show ya got *class*.

And a Betty could expect wonderment as she and her guy drove stoically down the boulevard... lookin' over thru that short side-light...more to give the observer a look *in*...than to actually *see out*... Yeah. On the sidewalk there was reciprocal wonderment that anybody so young could be so cool...so accomplished. So *cocksure*.

Williams might not have been totally right but he has one thing dead nuts: Customs are for date-night.

True to Tradition

Photo: Herbert Blomquest

Krafty '39

By Hop Up Staff – Photos by Buckshot Wilkins

Sid Cruce's 1939 Ford Convertible Sedan

If you're in Texas, from Texas, or been through Texas, you probably know Sid. You know... Sid Cruce from up in Waterford, near DFW?

Now, he and his lady Suzanne lean towards the custom side of the equation, as we could see fairly early on after we'd met him (Hop Up picked his taildragger '36 3W at the Lonestar one year). Then we heard about another one in his queue of rides...this '39 Vert Sedan with a kinda neat history. Now don't be mislead: we'd have shot the car anyway, as it has a Dick (Krafty) Kraft connection. Yessiree. That one. The cat who built 'The Bug' and started the rail dragster thing. Him. Kraft had sold the car to some unknown body in '48.

The '39 Convertible Sedan benefitted from roll-up windows, had very low production numbers, and what's left of 'em have been found and fixed, or restored. Finding this rig in 2002 was pretty lucky. Sid's lucky in a lot of ways, or so we've heard.

Our Pal Charlie Duran had brought the car in from Arlington, TX, where it had been for around 25 years. Before that it'd been a girl's ride to and from college for a couple years up in the North East...New York they said. (Good thing the Rollin' Boners never got hold of it.) And they say a sailor had got it from California to Georgia before that. But nobody was really keepin' track. They were just old cars, then, weren't they?

Well, seems Sid wouldn't let Charlie keep the thing, so he buys it, figurin' he'll make sure it got done his way; a way of which we approve. Now the cool part is when Sid sees an article on Stan Betz (Betz Speed and Color in Orange County), there's a picture of Stan's cousin (Kraft) in his 'vert, you know, back in the 'black and white' days, Sid commences a research project, finds Kraft

Custom 'vert turned out to be owned back in the day by Dick 'Krafty' Kraft. Today, Kraft and owner Sid Cruce turn out to be fast friends because of it.

Above: Tan and blood leather trim work is by Ray Spears in Granbury, Texas; top is Haartz cloth.

Below: 'Pillarless' design boosts the apeal of convertibel sedans; windshield garnish mouldings wer butted and welded, finishing some difficult engineering in the same high standard of the rest of the car.

and talks about some details he's noticed on the car. Well, Krafty certified it was indeed his ride. Bitchin'. A proven history linking the old Ford to a Pioneer car guy from the early days. They become good buddies, and Sid is off on another build project. The Coot has plenty time for it, because he can't find a job, and has all day to work on his stuff in a big, cool garage at his Rancho.

The body off...complete chassis resto with a ton of N.O.S. parts...flathead, punch some louvers, change the taillights, and lookie here, Bub. The primered hulk that had just been hangin' in various garages for 35 years or so...has now got soul. Again.

True to Tradition

Above: Balanced 239", Thickston Intake, Offy Heads and like that.

Below: Sid painted the car Mexicali Maroon after a body-off chassis resto. Of course a bunch of NOS parts were accumulated to make the car first class. We seem to have a bunch of NOS parts on the feature cars in the Annual, eh?

DELL—AAHL '36 Roadster

By Hop Up Staff – Photos by Brett Reed

Bill Dell was a kid with a bitchin' roadster. A '36. It was set up just like he wanted it to be, and he was lucky enough to have good taste and enough scratch to make it happen. That was a little before December 7, 1941.

He went to war, and Mom sold the car for $100 while he was gone.

So, he was a little bit unfulfilled when he came home (happy that the world had been saved from despotism and all), but still had a yearning for the one that got away, and it was not until the late 50s - early 60s that he got back on track. When he did, he recreated the car exactly like he had originally done it. Yeah, Buddy. Everything from the chrome

dash to the Buick parking lights. E-zactly.

Then came 30+ years of comfort from the car during which it gathered some naturally acquired patina; just a little...and then another separation was due.

Dell figured the car needed to be sold for practical reasons, and he also knew he had a prime bit of custom on his hands. A 'catch.' It had to go to a caretaker, not a flipper. Mike Aahl had been patiently watching Dell deliberate, and, probably because Mike is a Hop Up Guy (a Stroker McGurk Award winner and like that), Bill Dell granted Mike the custodial position of caretaker for the next (undefined) bunch of years.

The bitchin' car didn't require much in the way of fixin' and certainly wasn't gonna get any changin', so Mike's task is one fraught with pleasure and a sense of duty; duty to preserve and plan a hand-off some day far in the future...to some cat who is pre-qualified as a caretaker.

Could it be you, Young Fella? Don't be in too big a hurry.

True to Tradition

Left: Mechanicals were freshened up a bit and now '36 is in regular rotation with Aahl's other trad rides. Watch for a '40 coupe in Hop Up Special No.3.

Top left: Flathead has bonus goodies for spunk and curb appeal; Mike tends to have lots more of them in his Hayward stash.

Top right: Bone steering wheels and plated dashboards are finding their way in to Hop Up customs this time aren't they? Leather seat has 'wear' that only years of abrasion from jeans can cause! It's perfect.

Above: Accessory grille topper dates the build late 30s per Mr. Dell's scheme; was it an Eastern Auto Parts part? Whatever it is, it's genuine: Neither Mr. Dell or Mike Aahl would have a ringer.

Single Bar Flippers, Olds bumpers, spare removed, chopped roadster top, all prescription items from the early practitioners of the custom art. Not a taildragger, probably more precisely accurate to the period; 'nice to see them out there in both stances.

The Second Coming of the...

The 1948 TIMBS Special

By Hop Up Staff

We do hot rods and customs here...or should we say hot rods and customized cars? Yeah. Our typical customs are cars customized, changed, morphed, twisted and dreamt into our vision of what Detroit might have done with that subject.

A custom car, necessarily, is original from inception. It starts as a blank canvas...like the Timbs car.

There were lots of these things done, not all successful. Today we have jaundiced and conditioned eyeballs; sometimes we can be hypercritical of early efforts until we put them into their time context and begin to value the forward thinking of the designer/engineer. This one may not be for everyone, but it is

without doubt a top example, heralded in all the Bigs of the day: Motor Trend, Popular Mechanics et.al.

Norman Timbs was an automotive engineer who had Indy roadsters to his credit along with more mundane day-to-day accomplishments, and he was considerably taken by streamlining. It shows, huh? His custom car was to be the prototype for a limited series of cars reflecting advanced concepts in performance and aesthetics. They'd make a series of them and probably make some scratch along the way, too. Ever the disciplined engineer, Timbs thought it out, studied and researched. He did comprehensive chassis drawings that led to

1/4 scale clay models of the several body ideas, and finally a wooden model employing the favored elements.

We don't yet know the entire chronology, but 50 years later the car was a derelict in the High Desert of Southern California. Our Art Director, Marc D'Estout, saw it there and photographed the car over ten years ago, and was recently stunned to see it was being restored at Custom Auto in Colorado. Thus, this article. On its journey, the car seems to have been owned at some time recently by a Hollywood prop man who placed it rather fleetingly in "Gone in 60 Seconds." The custom was there for only 2 of the 60 seconds, though!

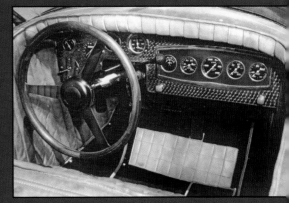

Soon after its movie debut, the car was at the Petersen Auto Museum Auction and wasn't making much of a hit with the bidders. Collector Gary Cerveny was there with his son and his father for a three-generation Father's Day outing, and, noticing no real activity, threw out a bid as kind of a 'priming' gesture. You know. Good will. Charity.

Damn if he didn't end up owning the car!

Later on at the auction, when Gary's Dad mentioned to his Grandson, "I pity the guy who bought that one," he was told, "We did, Grandpa!" Grandfather is an old-time sheet metal expert from the Skunkworks of Defense Industry fame and he was not impressed!

Motor Trend December 1949 was taken, as we are, by the complete-ness of design and function of the Timbs Special. Timbs was not a typical home-builder, rather, he worked as a race car and mechanical design engineer on Indy Cars and more. His personal project reflects that professionalism and advanced thinking. An 'opportune' bid at an auction found the car in the Cerveny family collection and finally at Custom Auto in Colorado for complete restoration.

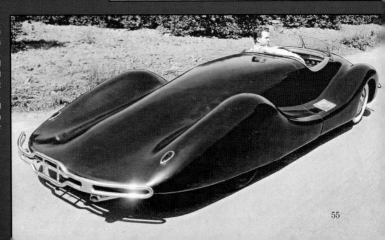

Gary relates that they tinkered with the car for a year or so in-house where most of their resto work is done, but ultimately decided that Dave Crouse was the man for the major job the historical car deserved.

And we got inside the inner sanctum of Custom Auto to see the progress and scoop the Bigs. The car is further along now, in fact probably done about the time this Annual is published. We'll follow up with finish shots in the next Special.

True to Tradition

Top: The original in-the-white build shot dramatizes design, metal work. Then and now, it's sometimes hard to put finish color on such art.

Right and below: 064 gage aluminum body is ready for color. Front half is static, while back half hinges, raises up hydraulically to access engine, axle, spare, tank, et.al.

Buick Straight 8 aft of driver. Diff is rigid mounted with swing axles and a buggy spring behind. Frame is 4" diameter steel tube.

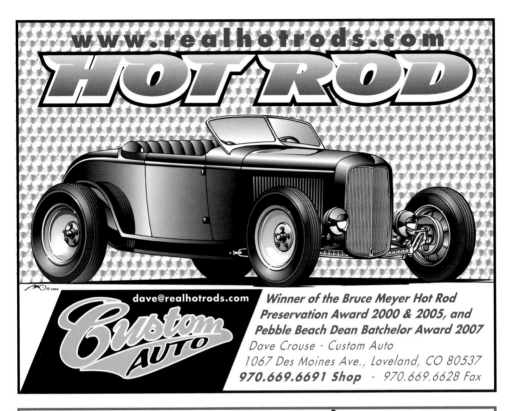

COACHCRAFT

In the late 30s, an aspiring actor from a wealthy family named Paul Planette wanted to stand out. He was rumored to be quite a ladies' man and an active player in the Hollywood scene. In a time when actors like Clark Gable had special cars built to their unique specifications, Paul did the same by commissioning Coachcraft (the craftsmen behind many of the Packard-Darrin vehicles) to build a custom Mercury roadster also known as the "door-less wonder" in late 1939 and early 1940. This one-of-a-kind Mercury Roadster was the first of twelve custom-bodied cars built by Coachcraft of Hollywood.

A couple of years after the car was built, Mr. Planette got into a car accident in which both the front and rear end of the car got damaged. He went back to Coachcraft to have them fix the car, but they passed the business on to fellow custom car builder, Jimmy Summers. Mr. Summers made major modifications to the car, including filling the nose.

Not much is known about the car from this time until the mid 1970s. Rudy Stoessel (founder of Coachcraft), Bill (son), and Anthony (grandson) remembered seeing this car sitting in a stream with water running through it around Temecula, California in the mid-70s. They were going to check the car out in order to restore it, but never stopped. Rudy was noted as saying, "There, the car shall lie..."

Fast forward to May of 1986, when my father and I (then 16) had a chance to check out a warehouse full of all sorts of goodies. We really did not know what to expect, but the experience was (and is still) unbelievable. We went to a large warehouse where the Brucker family stored most of their cars, parts, and tons of movie memorabilia. This experience alone is a story in itself. The Brucker family used to operate Cars of the Stars, Movieworld, and other movie related rental businesses. There were many, many cars throughout the property, most of which were used in movies or previously owned by movie stars. In the midst of all the cool stuff also lived an old man you may have heard of...Von Dutch.

Moving on... As my father and I walked through the dark basement I noticed an

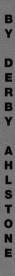

BY DERBY AHLSTONE

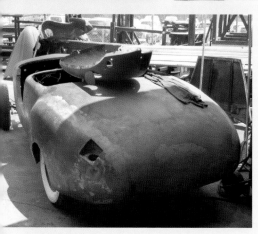

Opposite page: The profile was captured while on display at Art Center College of Design. Inset: 1940 picture of this "first" coachcraft car.

Top right: This father and son photo was taken the day the car was towed home.

Above center: These shots show just how rough the car was by the time it sat at Brucker's warehouse.

Above: Dissasembly and cleaning begins. Only now is the project's magnitude starting to register.

old custom car with 4 flat tires and a pile of junk on top. I pointed it out to my father, and he immediately said, "That is the 1st car Coachcraft built." He knew much about the car and its manufacturer based on his memory and vast literature collection. I told my dad we should buy it. He said no, but I asked how much it was anyway. My father still said no, so I bugged him all the way home. I asked my mom, and she said the same. Then in desperation, I checked my own bank account, and I had exactly enough to buy the car myself. My mother was still leery, but my father finally said, "It is his money, if he really wants to..." Well, I made the deal, and went completely broke in the process. I just knew that I did not want to tell my kids or friends later in life that I could have bought that Coachcraft car, but passed. If it wasn't me, I am sure it would have been someone else telling this same story. At that

Above and right: The process begins. Excellent metal fab and patch panel work was tackled by Bill and Shawn Denny. Chassis and 99A Flattie also underwent a full restoration.

Next page: Various shots of body prep, paint, wetsanding, upholstery, and reassembly show the level of detail lavished upon this historically significant custom.

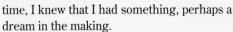

time, I knew that I had something, perhaps a dream in the making.

Well, 20 years of life went by, all the time waiting for spare time, extra money, and available space, which seem to never happen to us car guys. In August of 2005, I was selling literature at the Automobilia Monterey event. Occasionally, I would put an old photo of my car out in my booth to see if someone recognized it, or was interested in it. This time Bill Warner (Chairman of the Amelia Island Concours D'Elegance) noticed it and stated that he was planning on featuring Coachcraft as the marquis car builder for his 2007 event. I was pretty excited. This was just what I needed; a reason to get my car finished (or should I say started). I had no excuse now, and a perfect opportunity to unveil this unique car not seen in public since the early 50s, and both my father and me can talk about the car that did not get away...

A year went by and I still had not started on the car. Then in September of 2006, Mr. Warner formally invited my car and me to his event in March of '07. It would be quite an undertaking to restore a car from a "basket case" to concours quality in six months. I did, however, have most of the parts (thanks to my father) collecting them over the previous

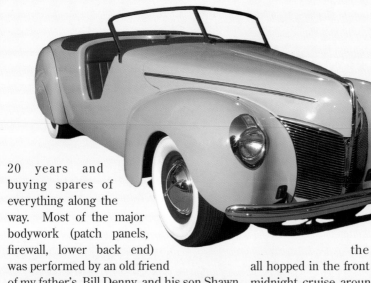

20 years and buying spares of everything along the way. Most of the major bodywork (patch panels, firewall, lower back end) was performed by an old friend of my father's, Bill Denny, and his son Shawn (both of Camarillo, California). They made quite a bit of progress over several months, but the show date was getting closer and closer. I knew that I could not miss this opportunity.

With only 22 days to go, I delivered the body to Steve Friedman, and the boxes of parts, frame, etc. to Justin Gosaynie and Nathan McNeil (all from Ventura, California). Once we all clearly understood how much was left to do to complete the restoration, there was some doubt as to whether the car would actually be ready for the Amelia Island Concours, but not in my mind. The onlookers pretty much had decided that it was not going to make it.

Steve completed the minor bodywork and painted the car within a mere 12 days. Jesse's Upholstery in Saticoy, California, completed the interior in a couple of days (with Jesse pulling an all-nighter, I might add). The drivetrain rebuild (by Williams Automotive of Ventura, California) came in on schedule, and she started right up.

Justin & Nathan really came through putting the whole car back together for the first time. We worked several late nights to make the schedule. No matter what issues came up, we, or should I say they, were able to resolve them. It was after midnight one night, and we finally got the car driveable. We all hopped in the front seat and took it for a midnight cruise around the block a couple of times. All we could hear was the engine idling down the road. In the back of my mind I was just hoping that it would not break down before we made it back to the shop.

The transport service was scheduled to pick my car up at 10:00 AM on Saturday. On this morning it was down to small details and sliding the front windshield glass into the frames. Quite a crowd of onlookers (including the car appraiser and insurance provider) had gathered this morning to see for themselves that we were indeed going to finish. When the driver showed up, I asked him to take an early lunch because it was evident we were barely going to make it. It took us three tries with everyone watching to slide the glass in. After the third attempt I hopped in the car, drove it around the block, and into the semi. What a relief! The car was on its way to Amelia Island...

At the Concours, the car was parked in the Ritz Carlton ballroom for the Coachcraft presentation. It also was driven in the Coachcraft and Fashion Show parades in front of the grandstand and announcer's booth. To cap an exciting weekend, the car also won an Amelia Island Award. I guess dreams do come true...

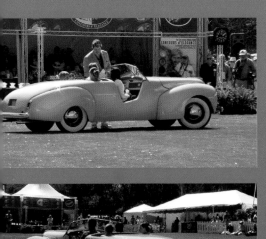

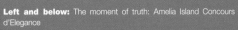
Left and below: The moment of truth: Amelia Island Concours d'Elegance

Bottom: On display at Saratoga Auto Museum with Coachcraft media show projected in background

The *Ron Gomez*

Sultry and Smooth

By Hop Up Staff - Photos by Rick Amado

The last West Coast Kustoms weekend in Paso Robles was a good one for Ron Gomez: He left with three awards for his Buick, including the Paso Veritas Award presented by Hop Up Magazine. And then there was the guy who greeted him on his way out on Sunday with a gracious compliment on the coupe. Ron asked his name, and the guy just said, "Oz." Ron's not out there for trophies, so the last 'award' (the verbal one given by an icon) was the most meaningful to him.

See, Ron was a Lowrider who 'got' customs pretty early on. His mind's eye kept drifting to early iron and the iconic '41 Buick 'verts with a Carson top. Us, too.

But a Model 44S coupe got in the way. He got the car about seven years ago and work started right away. Ron tells us that the project got going pretty well, was already cut and all, when at Ron's request it was politely critiqued by Jack Walker, who made some style recommendations. "That's how we used to do it," he pointed out.

The resultant modifications (handled-up by 100 MPH Club guy Fabian Valdez) made a finished art form out what was already a good effort. Fabian also recommended the paint color and texture; we can't agree more that it is the perfect touch for this fine custom.

Above: Sultry Buick custom is modified front to back and every panel in between. This is customizing that works, each element contributing to the complete design premise.

Right: A David Garcia rendering featuring a "High School Confidential" top resulted in overriding the plan to cut the top for a Carson treatment. Dragin Shop (Joe Garcia) did metal work; color is Emerald Green with a little pearl and eggshell clear, suggested by Fabian.

Buick

The car is completely done now, it's a daily driver (really, those words are over done but this sled is driven every day) and Mr. Gomez resists screwing with it this way: he is tipped over in the design and construction of a '39 Packard custom. That task ought to allow him to stick with perfection in the Buick.

Hop Up Honor. Stay Honor.

Top: Emerald and White interior looks 'period,' but on examination proves to be better than those early jobs, excellent layout and execution. We are real high on this ride.

Above left and right: Dash and accessory wheel are restored, appropriate to this kind of car; good taste, restraint. Longitudinal headliner is as nice as any we've seen.

Opposite top: Grille is sunk in, gravel pans are rolled.

Opposite bottom: Ron says, "About 500 of these Model 44S' were manufactured; they are all Chevy from the windshield back." How cool is that?

Race Cars

We thrive on the performance of our hot rods, and the 'Goal of Gow' is sought to the maximum in their purpose-built counterpart... The racecar.

Performance and the sheet metal cosmetology that masks the potential violence within...is the subject at hand. We'll look at a gorgeous restored dirt digger from the 30s, a drag rig (that sneaks on the street from time to time), and we will get a historical look at one of the least known connections between Muroc Dry Lake Racing and that icon of deadly dirt, Legion Ascot Speedway.

Racecar spelled backwards is... ? Yeah, Man... Racecar.

Photo: Curtis Patience

Nailhead Henry J

By Chuck Vranas

Regardless what day of the week it is, there's nothing more intoxicating than the heavy scent of nitromethane, alky, or Cam2 as it filters into the air at the drag strip. Some have been fortunate enough to have been regulars at the strip since they were youngsters with the long pit rows seeming like a home away from home, as they chowed down dogs chased with cans of root beer, while struggling to keep up with the announcer in the tower's minute by minute updates on just who was ripping up the track. For Buddy George of Wrentham, Massachusetts, his formative years were spent in the right places at the right times, especially considering that hot rodding and drag racing were in their rmative years when he was kidnapped into sacred brotherhood. Spending whatever sh he had from various chores he'd take re of around the house on little books, his ung mind was absorbing the latest rods and stoms from around the country, all of which the proverbial fire tuning him into just at made a gow-job hot. Walking through vis Square in Somerville after school, he uld always see one particular '34 Ford ghboy 2-door sedan that was packed with ot Flathead parked in front of Goff's Auto rts. This car embodied everything cool and uld have stood the test of time, especially day, if you caught it parked on any street rner. Suddenly the car disappeared from e landscape, causing the then 14 year-old panic, but relief was forthcoming when the r reappeared two weeks later channeled death in its same parking space. One day ile garage hopping with friends, he finally et the owner of that sedan, which opened a or that would forever change his life.

A friendship was struck up with Mike Amlaw, the owner of that killer sedan as well as Pete Jardim, who both welcomed Buddy into their inner sanctum of rodding and drag racing. Buddy recalls regular visits to the Sanford Drags in the late 50s, which obviously had an impact on him when he finally laid down some greenbacks to buy his first car at age 15, a bone-stock low mile '33 Ford three window coupe that would be a test-bed of countless mills (including his very first Nailhead) as time went by. Teaming up with a group of hardcore car owners, he joined in when they decided to rent the basement of Bowlby's Warehouse for 10 bucks each a month to house their projects. Buddy recalls that these guys were a bit older than he was, and that they always watched out for him,

Below: A refreshing change from the normal nosebleed stance that one has come to expect from a Henry J, Buddy's car is screwed to the pavement, which is a definite plus when dialing it in for a nice straight launch from the line. We're here to tell you first hand that the car leaves hard off the line and runs the track as straight as an arrow.

making them bigger than life heroes in his eyes. As the years began to creep by, the coupe changed hands, and Buddy focused in on a Henry J in '63 that he built into a wicked street racer that got its grunt from a 386-inch Nailhead. There was just something about Buick mills that grabbed his attention, which continued to morph into countless other projects, like a '58 Corvette that he hit New England Dragway with for the first time as a racer back in '66 powered by a 425-inch dual-quad Nailhead. Imagine the minds that were blown when that hood was opened in the pits! Time moved on, and Buddy spent time as a member of the Rikshaws, Custom Engineering Group, and Dominators, where all members were the real-deal who built their own cars and raced them, creating plenty of great memories along the way.

Fond recollections of that early Henry J he owned in the 60s always seemed to lurk in the back of his mind, since he never had the opportunity to turn it into a dedicated race car back then. A search thus began for a suitable starting point for the new project, which led him to Tulsa, Oklahoma, where he found a solid roller that would fit the bill perfectly. Having already been chopped 3-inches, it had an obvious evilness and a need for speed that would fit the bill perfectly. Once the car was home, Buddy was approached by Chick Brignolo of Norton, Massachusetts to fabricate a stout full-race chassis that could handle plenty of abuse. Constructed from 2x3 rectangular steel, it was packed with an independent front suspension complete with Strange coilovers and rack & pinion steering, while out back custom fabbed ladder bars and

Strange coilovers kept everything planted as Wilwood disc brakes all around bring everything to a halt. To give the massive M&H Racemaster slicks plenty to scream about once they hit the burnout pad, Buddy stayed true to his roots in assembling a killer '66 Nailhead to challenge the tree with. He worked with Gary Sharke at Performance Engine Shop in West Babylon, New York, who plotted a good course to follow with a 401 block which was bored & stroked to 426-inches and filled with an offset ground crank, Howard aluminum rods, Ross 9.5:1 slugs, and a custom-ground Schneider race cam. Topped with an Offy dual quad intake with a pair of Holley 625's by Jeff Lynch, dumping gasses through a set of Roy Idman fabbed headers, there is plenty of juice flowing into the final mix that includes a race-prepped '66 Buick TH400 by Don Robishaud, linked to a Brignolo narrowed 9" Ford rear end.

It's been a grueling 7-year project where it's all been about returning to his roots to create a race car that's got plenty of performance and attitude. Dialing in the body, Buddy radiused the rear wheel openings, added a rolled pan, and installed the early Chrysler taillights, while good friend Roy Costa completed the chop to the doors and helped out with the bodywork before Buddy laid down the temporary gray primer. A race car interior and rollbar was installed by Chick while the

wiring chores and many others were handled by Jeff Lynch. Hitting the strip to dial in the beastly Nailhead, Buddy has been able to prove that Buicks can still tear it up with a best 1⁄4-mile run of 11.67 @ 113 to date. Who could argue with that! As with all projects, there are loads of friends who team up to lend a hand, and Buddy wanted to say thank you to the following guys for their support in getting the Henry J ready for the strip: Tom Telesco, Dave Robson, Ritchie Cockerline, Karl Sheaffer, Joe Ouellette, Paul Pfeffer, and Garth Goodnight.

Above: The combination of a 3-inch chop along with the chassis dynamics that get it ever so close to the ground give this hop-up a look that's not easily forgotten. With a set of massive M&H slicks filling up the radiused rear wheel wells accented by the rolled rear pan and Chrysler tail lights the car is just plain bitchin'.

Left: Most people get a big surprise when looking under the hood half expecting to see a Rat or a Snake! Buddy's car is as serious as they come with a race-prepped 426ci Nailhead machined by Gary Sharke and assembled by Buddy strapped to the rails which dynoed at 343 hp and 458 ft/lbs of torque @ 4400 rpm. To be sure that the mill has plenty of go power, it was packed with an offset ground crank, Howard aluminum rods, Ross pistons, and a Schneider stick, while an Offy intake with Holley carbs gets plenty of air into the mix. The cool headers are the work of local craftsman Roy Idman.

Far left: Interior-Nuthin' fancy here just a hardcore work environment with aluminum and cage protection provided by Chick Brignolo, while Autometer gauges keep Buddy informed on everything that's happening under the hood.

Top: As badass as they come, the little Henry J is a definite giant-killer as it lurks at the line waiting for the Christmas tree to light up. Buddy is able to nail down some pretty impressive reaction times often leaving his opponent waiting around like they've stalled out...that is unless he red-lights or stages too deep!

THE KEHOE

Riley

SPECIAL

Photos by Rick Amado

This rig has been on these pages before, in an earlier incarnation. That was soon after Bob got the car, where he had stretched the body a few inches, fixed the mechanicals on it, and started to use it as the functional, historic artifact that it is.

Bob Kehoe is a 200 MPH Club guy. We mean, like, 13 Bonneville records and 10 more at Elmo. Season champion with Bruce Geisler in 1969. And more. There's cool street iron and other stuff to keep him busy, too, but after the above noted 'wake-up,' the sprint car wasn't maximized in his mind. It hadn't yet become the fulfillment of that Daytime Dreamin' most of us suffer. An' when you got that? Yeah, Pard: Ya gotta go back in. He did, and we think he scored... Big.

Coupled with Amado's photographic skills, the concourse quality car is poster, calendar, and TRJ material. Or Hop Up.

Yeah... Hop Up.

Above: Four-port Riley is a cross flow head, induction on the left, exhaust out the right and three valves per cylinder. These are rare, original, good speed parts. Engine done by Jay Steele at Taylor Engines has full pressure to inserts. Damascened firewall highlights the fine finish of the car. Back in the day there really were a few sprint cars finished this nicely.

Below: '29 Chrysler axle had to be converted to transverse spring. Hangin' it on the bulldog perch kicks the front out and down, and makes for that smart stance. "T" spring.

Above: More machine-turned metal, chrome, and leather by Whitey Morgan.

Below: The stance to which we refer. This is a fine car by any measure and from any perspective. Bob Kehoe, Dennis Webb (frame and body), Jay Steele, and Whitey Morgan can be very proud.

Above: Receptacles for 'bones are reminiscent of Miller parts copied by everybody who strove for refinement in race cars. Chassis is a two-springer. Lotsa race car chassis became the foundation of modifieds on the lakes in later lives.

ORIGINS OF

BY DAVID BROST

The origin of hot rodding is always an interesting subject. Like many things, there is never one source. People, places and the right timing all must come together. One such story is that of a native Californian, Paul Weirick, who was born near Pasadena in 1910. No one really knows when he became interested in racing, but by 1930 he had acquired a AAA racing license, owned and raced a small sprint car, and was aware of the 5/8th mile track in Lincoln Heights, known as Legion Ascot. Another favorite place of speed that attracted Weirick was Muroc dry lake.

During the mid twenties the AAA contest board held top speed time trials for various board track and Indy 500 cars. It was the closest place to Los Angeles for straight away speed runs. Official results for the fastest cars gained them sponsorship money and the knowledge that modification refinements had actually worked. In 1927 Frank Lockhart achieved an incredible two way average of 164 mph and one way of 171 mph on the dry lake with his 91 cubic inch supercharged Miller Indy car. This kind of excitement ranked right up with Charles Lindberg's flight across the Atlantic.

HOTRODDING

By the middle of 1931, Weirick had built a RAJO powered Model T hop up. This car was stripped down, lowered and utilized wire wheels. It may have been his daily transportation, and, like most other early dry lake competitors, he drove the modified to and from Muroc. In June and October of 1931 Paul was successful enough to win first place trophies. The only known recorded speed of Weirick's "T" was 95 mph in 1932. These roadster races may have been organized by either Earl Mansell or Gilmore Oil Company. Weirick's racing life continued to change gears during 1931. Early in the year Weirick teamed up with Art Sparks, and together they built a sprint car to run at Legion Ascot. This car became known as Poison Lil, one of the top winning sprint cars in history. Poison Lil's racing life spanned nearly two decades.

While most of the country was deep in the depression, a successful race team could make $1000 a week. However, many Ascot drivers ventured to Muroc to meet their need for speed. The thrill of moving at over 100mph on the dry lake was the only reward, as cash prizes were not awarded. People wanted to get their minds off the depression and turned to filling the stands at Legion Ascot, or making the trip to

Page 78: Muroc 1931. Paul Weirick's "T" hop up among other early dry lakes competitors. Note interesting fender on car at far left and everyone wearing heavy coats. **Inset:** Close up of "T" hop up. Paul at wheel. Car was equipped with RAJO head and licensed for street.

Page 79: Muroc 1931. Rear view of Weirick's "T" behind crowd. Gas tank sure hangs low. Hop up capable of over 90 mph.

Left: 1931 photo taken just north of Foothill Blvd. near Glendale. Paul Weirick (left), Art Sparks (right) with driver Arvol Brunmier who was known as the "Whittier Shiek."

Center: Trophies won at Muroc by Weirick during 1931. Car clocked at 95 mph by 1932.

Bottom: Poison Lil was a new race car when this photo was taken in spring of 1931. It was powered by one of the first Miller 220 four cylinder race motors.

Muroc. Tens of thousands showed at Ascot to see these guys battle each other, two and three times a week. The dry lakes would not see large crowds until after the war, but it was growing in popularity. Newspapers hyped up the circle track excitement by falsely creating drama and tension between drivers. Night racing became popular. Movie stars enjoyed box seats. "B" rated starlets presented trophies to the winners. Race themed movies and Saturday matinee serials were filmed at Legion Ascot using actual race cars and live footage. It was NASCAR of the 1930s and the way to make a living in racing was at Legion Ascot.

In 1932 Weirick and Sparks built "The Catfish," the first Indy car designed by engineers in a wind tunnel. To gain valuable Gilmore sponsorship, "Stubby" Stublefield and Weirick took the car to Muroc with the intent to set a new class AAA record. Weirick understood the conditions on the dry lake. The run needed to made early in the morning. Time was short, as they needed to get the race car to Indy. Special wheel covers and suspension fairings were fabricated just for the speed run. On the first attempt the car could not get up to the 6200 rpm needed to go 150 mph. The cam and spark plugs were changed, but it was too late in the day. Better luck prevailed the next morning as they set a new record at 147.355 mph for a 4 cyl. engine under 305 c.i.d. Unfortunately, the car only managed 14th place at Indy.

In that same year, Weirick and Sparks moved back west into a shop of their own at

Top: Muroc spring, 1932, prepping Gilmore Catfish for speed run. Car had 220 miller engine from poison Lil and Ford rear end and clutch. Truck at right oiled course to cut dust.

Left: The 1932 Catfish was Paul and Art's first Indy car. It qualified 25th at 112 mph and finished in 14th place. Car was sold to Fred Frame and raced another 5 years.

Below left: Two of Weirick and Spark's crew stand guard over the Glendale shop on Isabel St. in 1932.

Below right: Primitive as it may be, this shop built great race cars. Note the belt driven machinery.

Left: Paul Weirick making adjustments on Poison Lil, 1935.

Below: August, 1932. Poison Lil was a proven winner. Gilmore sponsorship allowed funds to chrome and paint car- blue fishgill (metallic) with red trim. Sparks is pictured at far left, Weirick in center and driver Kelly Petillo in suit on right.

124 Isabel Street in Glendale, CA. So much time was needed to run Ascot and develop the Indy 500 cars that Paul could no longer attend dry lake meets. By late 1936, Weirick and Sparks reluctantly parted company. Sparks went on to build race cars to compete with the Europeans, and Weirick continued to campaign Poison Lil until 1948.

It is amazing to consider how fast the hop ups and sprint cars were driven on dirt 75 years ago. It was not uncommon for sprint cars to attain over 90 mph and over 110 mph at Muroc in a hop up. A driver was harassed for wearing a safety helmet. There were no fire suits, and the cars provided nothing to protect the driver. These people worked with little more than two sticks to rub together. Even the best equipped race shops were primitive. They improved their machines by trial and error. Yet they created some of the most awesome purpose built cars of all time. They were pioneers of both motorsports, dedicated to going as fast as they dared.

It's about the iron.

BONNEVILLE
SPEED WEEK

60TH ANNIVERSARY

AUGUST 18 - 24, 2008

Be a part of 60 years of Hot Rodding History on the Bonneville Salt Flats

For more information contact:
Southern California Timing Association-
Bonneville Nationals Inc.
PO Box 10, Orosi, CA. 93647-0010
Phone: 559-528-6279   Fax: 559-528-9749
www. scta-bni.org

75 YEARS

Deuce

1932
2007

Colby

WALDEN SPEED SHOP PROUDLY CELEBRATES A LEGEND

Walden
SPEED SHOP

Visit Us! WALDENSPEEDSHOP.COM

Style

Uh-huh. It's that distinctive way in which right-minded car guys, *and gals*, live their car lives. It's their flair for 'correct execution,' their choices, and their conduct.

Or it's their heredity and the environment that, coupled with those right genes, made them the skilled fabricator, engineer, or driver that they became.

Hop Up *Style* can be most anything, so we try to corral it for you in one place with its indistinct definitions and grey lines, knowing that you know what we mean. You know why it's included, and why it interests you.

And you don't need to know a secret handshake. Naw... g'head and take in some Style. No thanks necessary: You're *in* 'cuz you're *kin*.

True to Tradition

Elmer SPATZ

"Uncle Elmer"
By Neal Jennings

Uncle Elmer didn't ever say much about his racing days, or anything else for that matter, but on occasion it was mentioned, and he did follow my dad's Model T speedster project closely. Unfortunately, Uncle Elmer passed on shortly before the speedster's completion. He never did share the pictures and articles of his racing days...those were found and given to my dad after his passing.

Elmer Spatz married Helen Jennings, my grandfather's sister, in 1936. Elmer was the proprietor of Palm Avenue Garage in Alhambra, California in the late twenties and thirties. He then owned and operated the Standard Motor Service in Temple City until his retirement in the 1960s.

From the newspaper clippings, we know that he raced at the dirt track in 1926 and 1927. He raced locally at Ascot as well as the Pacific North West circuit with the "California Speed Kings." This was a group of Southern California racers that went on tour with a promoter to the Pacific Northwest.

During the PNW tour, Elmer was involved in what was dubbed the "Deadly Dirt Track Duel." Elmer and fellow Southern Californian, Bob Parsons, had been quarreling for the last month. Each claimed the other had forced them off the track into the fence and other such mishaps.

Above: 1901-1986 - E.B Spatz, aka "Uncle Elmer"

Left: "Elmer Spatz of Los Angeles, shown in his speedy racer, will have it out with Bob Parsons of the same city in a special match race feature event of the automobile speed program on the Vancouver speedway.

Both boys are dirt track specialists and they will hit those turns at a dangerous clip."

Below: Spatz owned the Palm Avenue Garage in Alhambra, California, where customers could buy Gilmore products, Goodrich Silvertones, or even get a part welded.

"Took out seven 6" x 8" posts, this is the way I stopped."

Elmer characterized Bob as a "swell head" and Bob claimed that Spatz was a "smart aleck" youngster. The two agreed to race each other 'catch as catch can' on the track at Bagley Park (Vancouver, WA), immediately after the scheduled races were over that afternoon. The race between Spatz and Parsons was called in the fourth lap after a piston in Spatz's car broke, leaving the feud still unsettled. Later in the season, Elmer did go on to take the 1927 Dirt Track Championship of the Pacific North West. This could possibly explain the reason that his car carried the number one at one point. Two articles mention Elmer driving different cars. From what I gather the #1 car was the Brockman Special, as this article states, "Spatz entered in Ascot race. Driving the Brockman Special, the same car with which he copped the Dirt Track Championship of the Pacific Northwest, defeating Jack Ross."

If only Uncle Elmer was still around to tie this all together for us...

Above: E.B Spatz in front of Palm Avenue Garage, Alhambra

Right: The Glendale Special, after it came spinning out of the north turn and lost a right rear wheel... taking out seven posts.

Below: Elmer Spatz, looking fresh and "new," shown in his speedy racer, just before a test run.

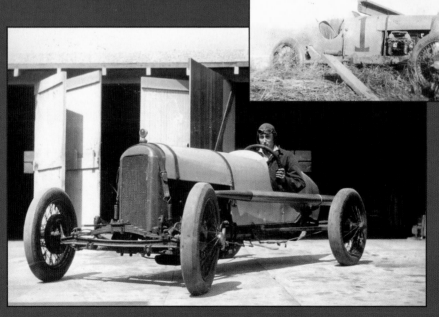

Veda Orr

by: Eric Loe

The Mother of Modern Hot Rodding

The first half of the twentieth century saw the development of the hot rodding activity and all its major facets. The foundations of dry lakes racing, circle track racing, drag racing, hot rod shows, car clubs, the speed equipment industry, and magazines devoted to the hobby had all been laid by approximately 1950. Anyone involved with the activities during those formative decades can be considered a pioneer. Whether they founded an equipment line, set a record, established a magazine title, ran a speed shop, hosted an event, or built and drove a car modified for greater speed or performance, all had a hand in creating the varied activities known as hot rodding.

One of those pioneers was Veda Orr, though while growing up in rural San Bernardino, CA, in the 1920s it is unlikely she ever entertained the thought that she would one day be considered as such. There is no evidence to suggest that she came from an automotive background, nor reason to believe she would have been encouraged in that direction, should she have shown interest during that period. Looking back through time it would seem that she was an unlikely candidate for such a title.

As a young adult Veda moved away from her high desert home and relocated to the Los Angeles area. She obtained a job at MGM Studios in Hollywood and began work in the Scenery Department. It was this move to Los Angeles that brought her into contact with the fledgling world of hopped up vehicles with which she would later be so closely related.

In 1935 Veda met Karl Orr. Karl had moved to southern California in 1927 from Kingston, Missouri, where he had been involved with track racing and race car building. He continued his automotive and racing activities in Los Angeles and joined the ranks of young hop up enthusiasts who made regular treks to Muroc Dry Lake for speed contests.

Veda and Karl hit it off and were married in 1936. Veda began accompanying Karl to his racing activities. Karl was a member of the "90 MPH" club at the time and Veda took on duties as an informal secretary at the club meetings. She also started attending the dry lakes meets.

Soon Veda began to rib Karl about participation in the time trials. She told him that anyone could do it; all they had to do was keep their foot in the throttle and their head down. The teasing began to get to Karl, and one day at a meet he decided to call her bluff. He suggested that since Veda was always saying how easy the driving looked that perhaps she should take the car through the course. She hadn't ever driven the car full throttle, but it was no time to back down. She pulled their Model A roadster into line, Karl buttoned down the tarp around her, and when it was her turn, away she went! After that she was hooked!

Left: Veda Orr from an article in Collier's Magazine, April 5, 1947. (artwork based on a David Peskin photo)

Above: Veda Orr's "Lakes Pictorial" originally came out in 1947. It is considered to be one of the first books devoted to hot rodding. A revised version named the "Hot Rod Pictorial" came out in 1949.

The precise date of the event is lost, but in later years Veda recalled that this first run through the traps occurred in 1937 at a Russetta meet put on by Ray Ingram. Regardless of the specifics of when and where, it is fairly clear that from then on Veda was a regular participant at the races and no longer a spectator. In the years to come she not only competed at Russetta meets, but at SCTA, Western Timing, and Road Ramblers trials at Kearney Mesa as well.

When she made the switch to participant, Veda was taking a bigger step than her peers in the driving ranks had taken on their first run down the course. The simple reason for this was that many of them would not have considered her to be one of their peers. Up to this point, an unwritten understanding had been adhered to, "Only The Men Would Participate!" The ladies were welcome to come to the lakes and watch, but not to be actual participants. For some this was probably a conscious desire, for others it was just as likely such an ingrained expectation that they might not have even considered otherwise (men and women alike.) By getting behind the wheel, Veda was breaking new ground.

Some accepted her directly (Esau Thun, who spent time in the 90 MPH Club and later the Albata Club with the Orrs, recalled that both clubs accepted her as one of them), others were thrown off by the unusual situation. After the charter meet of the Southern California Timing Association on May 15, 1938, the Throttlers club came out with a short-lived publication called the Associated Timing News. The first issue incorporated commentary on that first SCTA gathering and included a sharp criticism of the meet, which read, "How did Karl Orr's wife get to drive through? That was one of the most inexcusable blunders that we happen to know of. It is understood by this writer that

Above left: Veda with her '32 Roadster. (Esau Thun photo)

Above right: Karl and Veda made a good team! (Esau Thun photo)

Right: This 1947 photo is representative of the way Karl and Veda seem to have generally divided up the driving chores. Veda drove the roadsters (first the AV8, later the '32) and Karl drove various modifieds and streamliners bought from other racers, including Johnny Junkins modified, Ernie McAfee's "no springs" streamliner, and Bill Warth's modified, seen here. When the Orrs made the switch to track racing they sold these cars. The modified was sold to Bob Path and Chuck More, who added a sprint car tail and raced the streamliner class at SCTA, RTA, and MTA meets. The roadster had a short CRA track racing career before they sold it and it disappeared. (Esau Thun photo)

Opposite: '28 Ford Roadster Karl bought in 1929. Veda's early racing experience came in this car. It was this car Veda used to set the record in the short-lived "stock" class with a speed of 104.40 mph. The roadster featured many modifications, including reworked front fenders, '32 truck grill shell, various four cylinders before switching to V8 power, a custom dashboard and three seats out of a Ford Tri-motor airplane.

she is not a member of the 90 MPH Club. If Karl told the fellows at the starting line that she is (a member), he should be held responsible." Veda continued to run at SCTA meets, but was not included in the programs. The Road Ramblers were also unsure about how to handle the situation. In the results sheet for their January 8, 1939 meet they list, "Mrs. K.P. Orr," as a participant in a "'29A-V8" with a speed of 99.56 mph, but stopped short of listing her as a member of the "90" Club along with the others. Veda recalled that women were also unsure of the situation, often commenting to her that they wouldn't want to do what she was doing.

Through the period of the late thirties Karl had kept his job at the Del Ray Garage and Veda had continued working at MGM. However, Karl had in the back of his mind that he would like to open a speed shop. By 1940 the timing seemed right and the pair acquired the use of a small building at 114 Washington Place in Culver City, quit their jobs, and went into the speed shop business. For the next decade, the Karl Orr Speed Shop would provide their livelihood, as well as serve as a meeting place and source of information to the racing community in the years to come.

With the onset of World War Two, the organized racing came to a halt, and a majority of the participants went into the military and were dispersed across the globe. Veda and Karl kept in touch with as many of their friends as possible, with Veda writing numerous volumes of letters to the far-flung racers. Even with the efforts made to keep track of as many racers as possible, many became unaccounted for as time went by. Then, in late 1944, Wally Parks suggested to Veda that she expand her correspondence efforts into a sort of news letter and start sending it out to as many of the old association (SCTA) members as possible. The first issue of the result, entitled "SCTA News," was sent out in November of 1944 to 158 racers, both at

Top: Veda receiving her timing slip after a run in 1947. (Jack Stecker photo)

Bottom: Rear view of the modified Veda drove to speed of 131.07mph. Photo taken in Orrs' Culver City home driveway. Their '32 Roadster can be seen in background. (Bud Morrill photo)

Opposite page: Veda waiting in line to make a run. (Esau Thun photo)

home and abroad. The four-page paper, along with news of what various people were up to and a short classified ads section, warned the readers that it was their paper, and would only continue if they sent in material that would keep it interesting and viable. A request was also made that the paper be passed on to other members the recipients knew of, and that the addresses of those people be sent in to be added to the master list.

The newsletter was a big success. Veda received letters from all over the world with material for future issues. The racers also did as they were asked and passed the sheets on to others and sent in addresses. The result was that the newsletter became the vehicle for rebuilding the association and time trials when peacetime returned. It accomplished the task of reuniting a surprisingly large percentage of the old participants and brought new enthusiasts into the fold. It also encouraged the racers to start thinking about what they would do when the war was over.

When racing resumed, the Orrs were there to participate. Now Veda's name was listed in the programs along with the rest of the Albata members (she and Karl had moved to the Albata Club prior to the war). She finished 21st in the 1946 points race and 17th the next year. She continued to be the only female participant.

Veda continued to publish the paper after the end of hostilities. The name was changed in May of 1946, to California Timing News (C.T.News) in order to widen its scope. The paper continued to report news of the clubs and racers, publish ads for cars and equipment for sale, and report the results of all types of motor racing in the region. It also featured a photo page showing cars and racing action, showcasing the work of various artists, such as Gus Maanum, Tom Medley, and Wally Parks, on the cover.

With the success of C.T. News under her belt, Veda took another step in the publishing world. In 1947 she came out with one of the first books on hot rodding, Veda Orr's "Lakes"

Pictorial. The soft cover book focused on the high point cars of the 1946 SCTA racing season and featured a photo of each car along with a description of speed equipment and recorded top speed. There was also a section devoted to the artwork of Dick Teague, and a pre-war photos section. Two years later a "New, Revised" Pictorial was brought out through Floyd Clymer Publishing featuring most of the same material, but with a few photos added as well as a section devoted to track roadster racing.

By the final years of the 1940s Karl and Veda were shifting their interest away from dry lakes time trials and were focusing on track racing. They participated in both for a time, but soon decided to concentrate their time and effort on full time track racing. The next dozen years saw them traveling around the country campaigning sprint cars.

They returned to California in the early 1960s and settled in the town of Canyon Country. There they did what they already knew well; they opened a speed shop in Mint Canyon alongside the old route to the dry lakes from L.A. They ran that shop for some time before retiring and moving to the San Diego area. Karl passed away in 1988. Veda followed him one year later.

In 1984 the Southern California Timing Association created the Vera Aldrich Award to recognize women whose efforts have furthered the cause of dry lakes time trials. It is not surprising that the charter recipient of the award was Veda Orr. During her lifetime she was one of few people who could claim to have participated at the dry lakes during the formative years of the sport (and set a record), been one of, if not the, primary character in the effort to keep the SCTA alive during the war years, been involved with the running of a speed shop, and one of the progenitors of the publishing industry devoted to hot rodding. Coupled with the fact that she did all these things as a woman at a time when women were not expected to be involved with rodding activities, these accomplishments make her a true trailblazer who not only helped the cause as it was, but also opened the door for a wider spectrum of enthusiasts to participate in the future. Veda Orr was a racing pioneer among pioneers.

Hot Rod Kulture

**Photos and words by
Jack Butler**

Most know of the excitement and energy that generated the post World War II interest in Hot Rodding in Southern California and elsewhere in the country. This energy and interest was a release of emotion, training and passion that erupted after years of conflict and emotional tension. This interest ebbed and flowed over the years but has never fully disappeared. Several years ago it started to re-emerge in the form of commercially produced cars and the rekindled interest of former Hot Rodders from the 40s and 50s in keeping their youth interests alive. Having outgrown or bypassed their interest in building their own cars, this work was outsourced to shops and garages that specialized in this activity. The commercially produced

Hot Rod was commonplace, as were the parts that were use to produce such vehicles.

A counter culture evolved within the community as a reaction to this "standardization" of creative activity. Individuals who had interest in, and a connection to, the "Old School" style of rodding and the "backyard mechanic" philosophy of "Build it yourself" started to evolve into a community of like-minded enthusiasts. Their cars were unique, individual and not always safe, but they were Hot Rods! Self-built, self-driven, these cars were not built for shows or trophies... they were all driven a lot, some daily. The car represents the owner, and the owner represents the car. This "attitude" is what first attracted me to the culture and to the desire to document it.

My own passion for these cars and my interest in the honesty and intensity of the individuals from this lifestyle are the primary motivations behind my project. The concept of using a super wide pinhole camera is philosophical as well as aesthetic. The practice is "Old School" traditional photographic practice, and the super wide angle of view gives me the ability to emphasize specific aspects of the individuals and the cars. In particular, it allows me to monumentalize the aspect of exaggeration.

Above: Michelle & Vern

Opposite, clockwise from top: Psycho; Michelle & Bob; John-Creeps; Kazu, Shinya, Ash, Ichi; Aaron Kahan's ride.

TALES OF THE OLD HOP UP
Where'd it Come From? Where'd it Go?

By Spencer Murray, who was there.

In 1951 a timid attempt was made to explore the hot rod and custom car phenomenon by a ubiquitous little magazine bravely called HOP UP. Bravely, for the moniker was west coast slang for a modified car and might not be familiar in other regions. The folks behind the attempt were hoping their meager offering would bring this little-known side of motorsports to an audience which would plunk down a monthly 15 cents – or better yet, $1.50 for a full year. It is interesting with over a half-century's hindsight to recount some myths and misconceptions that surround the little-heralded birth and gradual fading of the current HOP UP's ancestor, its rebirth exemplified by the copy you're reading.

Above: The HOP UP gang in '53 at a rare hosted luncheon near the Glendale office. Clockwise from editor Dean Batchelor seated at left; ad manager Jack Caldwell, unnamed secretary assistant, art director Lou Kimzey, partly hidden photographer Ralph Poole, publisher Bill Quinn, Spencer Murray (in mid-bite) and secretary Mabel.

Right: Author Spencer Murray's '49 Chevy custom by Link Paola at the 3rd annual Oakland Roadster Show in 1952, where it took 2nd place behind Joe Bailon's '41 Chevy "Miss Elegance." It was featured in HOP UP for June '52, then again in September, which led to his joining the magazine staff in January '53. There were only three classes in the early Oakland shows: hot rods, customs and antiques. Spencer was no stranger to customs, having had a Carson-topped '41 Ford in 1943, a ditto Chevy in '44 and , after WWII, a '46 Chevy fastback with full-length Jimmy Summers fenders.

1951

It began in the offices of Road & Track, by Enthusiast's Publications, Inc., tucked away in the Glendale, California building of a commercial printer who, among other work, printed R&T. Dwelling on foreign iron while basking in SoCal sun at the center of the rod and custom movement seemed ludicrous to some staffers, and they felt R&T should add stories about local cars and happenings. After no little urging, publisher Oliver Billingsley grudgingly agreed, but with a proviso: let the detractors produce a separate issue, a half-size magazine of only 5.5 x 8.0 inches. It would have only 48 pages including the cover and, with content prepared by R&T's people in their spare time to eliminate buy-out expenses, costs would involve only printing. The expenditure would be offset by ad sales to local speed merchants.

So that first HOP UP wasn't really a bold move, yet it satisfied those who felt that rods and customs might one day grow into an important segment of the automotive hobbyist scene. But the publisher remained skeptical that even a low-dollar test was worthwhile, so a paltry few copies were run off with a cover date of July. When it was found that the magazines were quickly grabbed up, thousands more were printed, but with some editorial changes and page shuffling. This brings us a myth regarding HOP UP's birth. Because of the time between the initial printing and the full-bore second, the cover date was changed from July to August (though "Vol. 1, No.1" appears in both).

Left: This is the infamous NHRA ad that appeared on page 40 for July 1951 but was replaced with other material when the NHRA saw that the little magazine's editorial direction might conflict with Hot Rod. Wally Parks was boss of both. Charter members got a windshield decal, membership card, member's manual and full association privileges for $2.00!

Below: Visual proof that two almost – but not quite – similar issues of the inaugural HOP UP were printed. The July printing was small for a newsstand test to judge if such an awkward-size magazine would sell. It did, so the cover date was changed to August, alterations were made inside and a full-tilt printing was ordered. HOP UP was off and running.

1952

The magazine was maturing by its second year. Customizing how-tos and do-it engine mod stories improved, and while such exotica as the Indy 500 and race car-building sometimes appeared, boats and motorcycles were thankfully gone. Articles in general were better written, thanks to Dean Batchelor's insistence on quality and accuracy. At the end of the calendar year Batchelor asked if I'd consider leaving Link's Custom Shop to work at the magazine. It was an easy decision and I joined HOP UP right after New Year.

1953

My start date was January 5th, my 26th birthday, and I began at $35.00 a week. Major changes would occur at HOP UP this year. Circulation and ad revenue, limited by the awkward size, had reached a plateau, but growth was necessary for revival, and something had to give. HOP UP had survived childhood until the last small-size for February, then became an adult in March when it appeared as a full-size magazine. The famous Hirohata Merc graced the enlarged cover, and the new size mandated a price increase to 25 cents. Results were immediate when our small but dedicated readership responded. Horror of horrors! Bring back our little HOP UP! It would have been physically impossible to resurrect the small size, so just as HOP UP had been the stepchild of R&T, a brand-new pint-size magazine was born. It debuted with the May issue, and to avoid hiring new people, Quinn assigned it to me without lessening my HOP UP duties. After a short debate we named the new magazine Rods & Customs, but dropped the plurals starting in June.

1954 and Beyond

Emphasis on HOP UP's title continued to decrease while the tag line Motor Life increased, chameleon-like. Editor Hill was gone by February and replaced by Don Werner; a switch from a true hot rodder to someone befitting the magazine's more adult status. Quinn's two magazines continued to grow, and by April Motor Life dominated the cover with the small sub-title Formerly HOP UP and Motor Life below it, but which would later disappear altogether. As time went on, what had once been HOP UP but had become Motor Life was folded into Motor Trend because of their similar content. Rod & Custom would continue, as we all know. HOP UP was gone, the first 20 'little-pages' issues considered its golden era, but it had carved a memorable niche in that special age of the hot rod and custom car. I truly hope the present resurrection of the fabled title does as well.

Acknowledgements

Profuse thanks are due the following individuals who so graciously helped when my memory lagged. Photographer Ralph Poole, whose images of those great cars of the Fifties will always be treasured, and who went on to build his own publishing empire. Jane Barrett, Road & Track magazines librarian and walking encyclopedia, who rules over a vast collection of automotive history. And especially Greg Sharp, who holds down the envious job as curator of the NHRA Wally Parks Motorsports Museum. Ask him about the photo of the "Notre Spassing" sign that I gave him 30 years ago.

Spencer Murray

if it's hopped up, it'll be in HOP UP

DEREK BOWER'S

BARN FIND

By Hop Up Staff – Photos by Rick Amado

Yessiree. They say they're 'still out there; and this one...not in a barn out among a bunch of cornfields, not in a warehouse surrounded by Packards and Stutzs...nope. This one was just in the neighborhood.

A guy approached Derek while he was loading a 'for sale' patina'd deuce roadster on the trailer at LA Roadsters Father's Day swap. "I know where there's another one o' them."

He sure 'nuff did.

Story, as we get it, (right or wrong, close or far, we're stickin' with it) is that in 1948 a Hollywood producer had built or bought a hot rod for his kid. The kid turns out to be a dork and doesn't like the hot rod, so it gets parked. When a house painter that worked

the Hollywood Hills area was brushing the house in 1950, he inquired about the roadster and was able to buy it.

He drove it some and got two tickets for no fenders, which were signed off after he installed the bobbed Model A fenders. Then some time in 1953 he got a ticket for no front fenders. The rig got parked again.

In '57, the painter's grandson turned 16 and 'stole' the car one day, drove it to the corner and was afraid of it. What is it about simple hot rods? Parked again. In 1959, the family moved from Alta Loma to Long Beach, took the car with them and pushed it in the garage. A wheel never turned again – 48 years - until Derek pushed it out in June of '07.

Amado's photos tell the story of the car, and Hop Up will follow up later with the details of its new life with the Savant.

It's about the Iron

Previous page, above, and below: An artful collage of Amado's photography makes you want to feel the texture of the shell, wheel, pitman arm, fender. Betcha Derek walks over once in a while and strokes this one accross the eye-brow the way we less lucky guys do our own treasures.

ANTIQUE

By Hop Up Staff – Photos by Peter Vincent

There's a place to go for parts in Southern Cal that's almost under the radar. Oh, they advertised like everybody else back when the Model A restoration boom was big (in the 60s or so) and they had a hot rod and hop up parts division that has been one of the real constants in our curriculum down here, like...forever. Antique Auto Parts, Specialty Automotive and PSI Inc., were all names for the outfit in Rosemead, where the late Gene Scott and his protegé Jim Gordon held court for the cats who were fixin' up hot iron the traditional way.

The decade-long trends came and went, but Gordon stayed. Many didn't know

what he stayed with. Well, he stayed in the same place. He stayed with tradition (Hop Up style). And he stayed there with an accumulation of parts that will make you short of breath: Head-shakin', jaw-droppin' awe-struck...dazzled...short of breath.

Lots of junk is for sale. Some is not. And some has not even been inventoried. See, entire truckload lots of genuine and N.O.S. parts were accumulated over the years, bought on spec, and warehoused; left to age like fine wine, and kept safe while the market ascended to the moment where the commitment to the storage is rewarded by attrition in the parts world, appreciation,

AUTO PARTS

Opposite: One of several engine rooms behind the scene...where nothing is for sale!

This page: More precious hard parts than you can shake a Winfield cam at, plus ephemera going way back and all the way up to a River City Reliability Run poster! It's a cliché to call these places 'Museums,' but this one captures the history of our journey through the actual artifacts of the ride. That's a Museum to us.

supply and demand...and like that there.

Jim is the reverent custodian of all this, and, far from mercenary, he has the disposition that it's cool stuff, stuff that should ultimately be distributed to the worthy, not just the wealthy. It's his long term goal to make the parts get where they belong, saving the day, ending the search for some tipped-over Ford guy like you.

So, when you call Jim looking for that rare doo-jobbie for your '38 Whatchacallit, he'll know right away if the part is available. He'll price it fairly, and you may get to pick it up and look around and give the place a visual 'scratchin' of the surface.' But don't ask for a tour. We got pics right here of the only time that was gonna happen!!!

An' you're right: It happened because Jim Gordon is a Hop Up Guy.

What's in your garage?

Above: It'd take more than a few visits to hear all the stories, learn all the provenance of the items in this trove; we're willin' to go back and try.

Opposite top: Don't guess we have to identify the items in this beautiful red stack, now, do we? Refer to your 'to do' list and call Jim.

Center: Some of this booty slips in to the art area here. Patterns. The original patterns for things like Cragar heads. The original patterns. Holy Moly.

Bottom: Axles, housings, torque tubes? "Yes, sir. What year was it you wanted? OK. And how many of 'em was it you needed?"

Lil' STINKER

'32 Five window Coupe

Vintage Photos by Richard "Speedy" Gunsaulis

Jez Hoye acquired a '32 5W that apparently had a past. Pacific Northwest to Canada to Jez in UK...he'd seen old mag articles on it, knew it had spent most of it's life in Spokane, Washington...and wrote to Hop Up.

The Spokane connection made us call Paul Bos, recent Cali transplant to Idaho, right across the border from Spokane... and he knew a guy. (Bos always knows a guy. Ed.) That led to John Gunsaulis and the great story of his pop, Speedy, and the attached words, co-authored by Jez and John.

How'd Jez pick Hop Up for the pleasure of presenting his story? Let's read on and see.

Above: Lil' Stinker getting a fresh flathead at NAMCO

Opposite above: An old Hot Rod hits the streets again, now terrorizing England. Note the spare tire cover not done yet.

Below: Vintage show snaps; left-1959, right-1955.

I had sold a '27 T and been on an exhaustive search for a new ride, when I came across the Holy Grail on an internet classified: A fully fendered "B" 5 window. It looked like a very 70s style rod with two wide mag wheels, and a high stance. But as I read on, something got my attention. It read "Ex-feature car from the 50s," and I started to imagine what this car might have looked like back then. I e-mailed the seller, who informed me that the car had been featured in Rod and Custom in 1957. It now had a 302 dropped in, but not fitted or running. The owner was very helpful, and arranged to get the car transported 900 miles to my shippers. In the meantime, a friend found the original R & C it was featured in. It was November '57, the

"32 issue" also featuring the Tony LeMasa roadster and Neil East coupe. My coupe had a name "Lil' Stinker," and had been built by a guy called Ray Peternell, who was a member of the Dragins of Spokane. There it was with whitewalls and Moons instead of the mags, and I couldn't believe my luck, as the Hot Rod gods had smiled on me.

Within 3 weeks the car arrived in England virtually rust free, still wearing the original white tuck and roll interior and pinstriped dash with Stewart Warner gauges. When I got the car home, I spent ages going over it. It was THE car, in the article, in my garage! The car's chassis and brakes were gone through and made sound; we then fitted steelies with wide whites and Moons discs as it originally

had. I then re-wired it and had the roof insert replaced (apparently blew out on the way to shippers). Lil' Stinker was back on the road!

After driving the car for a few months, the 302 was falling apart, and it got me thinking the car should be returned to its 1957 R & C spec. Lil' Stinker went to a garage called North American Motor Co. A new Flattie engine was build up with a hotter cam, Offy heads, Edelbrock 3 carb manifold, and new Stromberg 97s. It was then fitted to a T5 box with an adapter. We tried to work out the colour of the engine from the black and white pictures and decided to paint it Old English White (basically cream) to match the firewall. The boys at NAMCO thrashed for a month to get the car finished for a show in August called "The Hot Rod Hayride." When I went down to collect the car on the Friday morning of the show I was overwhelmed by the high standard and period finish of the work. The car finally looked just as it once was, and it now drove great. Lil' Stinker won the 'Hot Rod of the Weekend' award, which is in the spirit of the event.

Since then we have buffed and polished the old paint, and a friend of mine, Neil Melliard, an excellent pinstriper, has re-striped it from what we could see in the old black and white pictures. But on looking closely we could see the car had been re-painted some time ago, and it had been panel striped, so with a bit of artistic license, he went for going over what we could see. I also had the pleated spare wheel cover remade.

It was then sign written with a club logo, but instead of "The Dragins" of Spokane Washington, it now shows "The Vultures," of which I am a member, as a little history update.

Cheers,
Jez

Ray Pernells "Lil' Stinker" was a fixture along Highway 395, between Spokane and Colville. His house was one of those places that has so much interesting stuff around it that you can't focus on one thing as you drive by. The only difference was at Ray's house, all the pieces were off '32 Fords: Part of a Tudor here, and half a five Window over there. It was amazing. But most of all "Lil' Stinker" always stood out. Sometimes when you drove by, it was peeking out of Ray's garage, and other times it was in the front yard covered in snow. I loved stopping by to see it. The car was, and still is, the real deal. Surviving the Eighties with very few modifications was hard enough for most rods. but here was one that looked just like it did when it was in Rod & Custom in '57. The salt flat discs, the winged speedo, and the chrome frame horn covers...I loved it all. The only real difference was in the mill. Ray had pulled out the flattie and dropped in a 289 at some point, but that was easy to overlook. When it was inside the garage, "Lil' Stinker" was kept company by a 1932 three window, '31 roadster and a '32 Tudor. All on a dirt floor covered with vintage Ford parts. It was like stepping back in time. Ray loved that car. He once told me that "Lil' Stinker" was the only thing that he really trusted.

Around 1953, Dusty Rhodes actually brought the little Ford five window to the Spokane area.

At that time, it was powered by a 303 Olds with 6 carbs, and painted a metallic orange crush. Dusty sold the car to Don Rohrer in 1955. Together they pulled out the Olds motor in Dusty's mother's basement and installed a flathead. From my understanding, it was Buddy Brannon that actually named the coupe "Lil' Stinker." He added the running board covers, with the Dragins logo, and spare tire cover. He also had Art Santarosa paint the car red. The car changed hands several times before Ray bought it in 1957, each person adding a little of what eventually became "Lil' Stinker." My father, Richard 'Speedy' Gunsaulis, and Ray had been friends since the 50s and were in the Dragins Car Club together. He often talked about Ray picking him up from high school in the coupe when the R&C article came out, and how much that meant to him. That favor was repaid when someone broke into Ray's garage and stole the grille, running board covers, and spare tire cover off the car. When my dad found out what happened, he took Ray a new Deuce grille shell. It's hard for me to look at any five window hot rod without thinking of "Lil' Stinker." For me, it set the bar that I judge all others by.

John Gunsaulis

Archives

In case you think you were born too late, and always kinda yearned to live it out in black and white like we said up front, then...tune in, Bub.

As usual, the boys have elected to lay their treasures upon Hop Up, keen on the idea that viewing by 19 who **get it**...will be more meaningful...and have more cache...than broader distribution to the **unwashed**.

This time we got stuff that's just a black and white version of y'all: it's Hop Up Guys and Gals and their familiar iron laid out in grays and sepia tones. So, mute the color, hop up on that workbench and...yeah...it's the weekend...grab yourself a cold one. We're goin' in.

en hopup veritas

Photos: Art Chrisman Archives

From "Bert's" Brownie

By Jay Ward - Photos by Herbert Blomquest

Bert was a high school senior in 1946 when he heard word about what would be the first SCTA meet after the war. He grabbed his Kodak Brownie, and with buddy Blackie Garrett riding shotgun, he drove his '36 Ford Phaeton down that Friday night...

Bert still remembers sleeping on the lake bed and waking up to the sound of cars lining up and taking off down the dry expanse. He recalls details of those early days with great detail and clarity. Now enjoy viewing these never before published images from Bert's Brownie, along with a few of his comments...

Bottom left and right: Shown here twice is Jack Calori's '29 A "dual purpose" street/race car with the off color hood and Frenched front license plate. It was running a friend's race motor that year, hence the hasty need for a hood to meet SCTA rules. The car would return the following season with a 3 piece hood and its trademark upswept side pipes (also see page 119). It was common to see mismatched tires front to rear, as wheels were swapped to change rear end ratios. (ed- like a poorman's quick-change!)

Last Fall, Mike Calleria was checking out vintage scooter tin down south where he met his friend's 78 year old father in law, Herbert Blomquist, who was there helping with a housing remodel. This buddy stated that Bert was "really into the same sort of hot rods you are" back in the day, and that Bert used to take a lot of photos at the dry lakes in the 40s. That's all Mike needed to hear!

He took Bert out to see his '41 Ford in the driveway and showed him the hopped up flathead hidden inside. A spark reignited in the old hot rodder's heart, and after lengthy conversation, Mike offered to scan Bert's personal hot rod photos taken many years ago. So the story began...

Top left: This '36 3 window had been racing at night when it hit a trench dug by a farmer. The car fire lit up the whole area.

Top right: This car was driven to the lakes packed with 4 girls! The chopped '41 Chevy Fleetline had 20 coats of smooth, bright orange lacquer paint.

Opposite bottom: Hopped up Buick straight 8 from Porterville, CA.

Bob Badon's Scrapbook

Via Coy Thomas

Our Pal Coy Thomas is a prolific archivist of photos and history in our chosen field. His contributions to Old Cars Weekly and other print products are well known and pleasantly anticipated.

He recently spoke to another Hop Up Guy, Dale Seaholm, and they thought that these Bob Badon photos would be a good fit for Hop Up Archives. We agree.

Coy wrote:

Hi Mark, Please find enclosed some photos and items pertaining to Bob Badon.

I think you'll find this stuff interesting - I only wish Bob was still alive. He was a tough old Marine (Semper Fi. Ed). He passed away a year ago, but luckily, I was able to get all his pictures on a CD - Enjoy!

About four years ago I recorded Bob on video talking on his days of racing - great stuff, I miss the Old Legend.

Rust is gold,

Coy Thomas

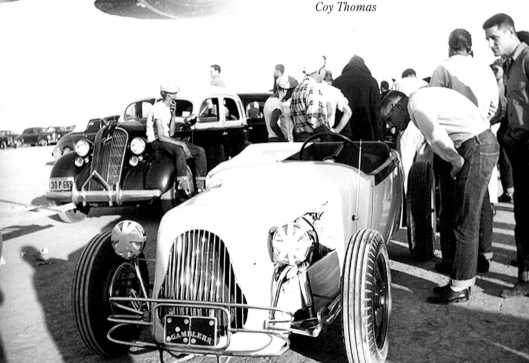

Bob was a member of the Sidewinders of Glendale, CA He ran with Rollie Free, Buddy Fox, Bill DeMott and the crew at many tracks in So. Cal. More personal fame came at the drags (see next page).

Lower left: Very unusal front engined bellytank

Lower right: Jack Calori's iconic A roadster. (Whitewall tires imply this photo was after the car was sold to dentist Bill Potts.)

This Page: Familiar players at the lakes, including Capana Marmon and So Cal belly tank, are unique in that they come from Badon's lens/ perspective.

Bottom: Tony Capanna 16 cylinder Marmon Roadster

Middle: That must be Rollie Free; Famous Bonneville pose, but he's not wearing the trunks !

Next page: The dragster in color shows two iterations of the Fox and Badon Dodge which, once, took top time of the day of 134.73 at San Fernando in front of "800 spectators."

ED JUSTICE JUNIOR

Shooting at 14- News at 11

The magic of capturing a moment in time, a piece of history to be relived later, always appealed to me. I guess when I would look at the images I shot, at a later time, it gave me a feeling of ownership of that moment in some small way. In particular the "rawness" of a black & white image was at the top of the list.

Growing up in a family with strong roots in the automotive and racing field was the perfect match for my future dreams. After all, attendance at weekly racing events with my dad was already happening. Why shouldn't I take my camera along? That led to, why

Above: The right place at the right time. Wouldn't you be smiling?

Below: The MOB is shown warming the tires in front of the crowd at Irwindale. As a spectator, the 'good ole days' just couldn't be beat. Look how close they let you get back then.

Above: What strikes me as interesting in this photo is the closeness of the roll bar to the drivers' helmet. This was before it was realized that a roll-bar could hurt you by being too close!

Below: Mike Sullivan was a tough competitor in the fuel altered ranks. This behind shot at the Winternationals shows the view many of his competitors had when racing him.

Top left & right: Fuel altereds came in all shapes and sizes, but they all had the motor perched totally exposed up front for the whole world to see and enjoy. Now that's racing!

Above: As seen in this photo from the 1970 Supernationals at Ontario Motor Speedway, large crowds at the drags are nothing new.

Left: Yes they would let us stand on the track in front of the cars. Then the lawyers showed up and the party was over.

shouldn't I sell my pictures for money? Which led to having my pictures published in the top magazines at the time and supplying photos to the drivers and teams themselves. Pretty heady stuff for a naive, but obviously bold, teenager. To put this in a racing perspective, I was 14 in 1969. This was the first year for funny cars to run at the NHRA Winternationals. The next year, 1970, was the first year that the funny car class was contested season-long in the NHRA. At the time I had no idea what I was actually witnessing. Here almost 40 years later and we do know what we witnessed back then. Over the years, I've shot both major and minor motorsport events around the world. From tractor pulls held in the back "40" of some farmer's field to the Indy 500 for over 30 years. I really enjoy going back through the files; heck I might even do a book or two. It seems people are interested in this stuff.

E. J. Jr.

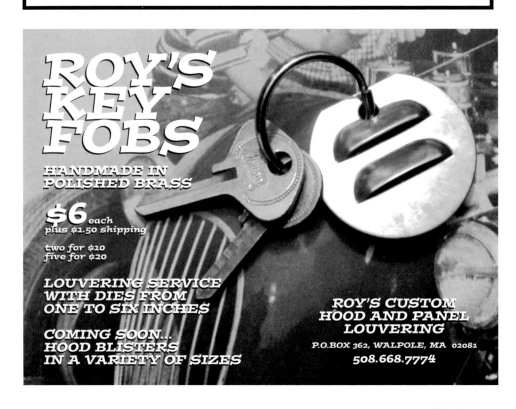

Art Chrisman

By Hop Up Staff

Yeah, we know him. Somebody has to. It's not that he's inaccessible, but when you're that important of a name, people might kinda hang back. And when you don't court the fame, ya don't curry the attention...an' ya don't posture yourself conveniently near the camera...like some of them...you can get missed. But we caught his ass, and he had his ol' scrapbook with him. It's Art. He's a Hop Up Guy. No, really a Hop Up Guy, like about the first member of the Hop Up 200 MPH Club, ya know? Yeah, Buddy.

One thing that was apparent when we went to lookin' at his pictures is that they're all good, mostly pro-shot, 8x10, and we realized: Yeah. Everything he has done in the hobby has been in front, first, fastest, and most clever or something. And all of that was obviously notable to writers and photogs, so we don't have any of those smallish Kodak moments and un-centered amateur things

Above: Art, his brother and dad in front of the shop where it all began. The Model A was done there and the guys attacked their passion under the tutelage of their father. Looks like the sedan on the left might have had a juice brake conversion already, huh?

with pinking-shear edges. We had lots to work with, but very little space to do it.

We settled for the few attendant photographs here, and as usual, some pearl-ish, laugh-punctuated stories to go with damned near every image here. And more laughs for the ones we didn't use. And for all those still in the accordion file. And the box.

Like the one with the track roadster and the boys standin' around it: Rosie drove it. It was Art's engine and Harold Miller's car. The track in Porterville was muddy, not too well groomed and Rosie said, "Engine's no good." Now, Art thought it was making too much power in the slick, so he didn't tell Rosie but he disconnected a plug wire. When Rosie came in after qualifying, cussin' and stompin' around saying, "It's really bad now, hardly runs!" That's when they told him he just set the track record and qualified on the pole for the main event!

And who knew Chrisman had a genteel side? A custom? First real car a '36 Ford Fordor? Yikes. But it ran, too. On opening day of the first Santa Ana drags, Art was sitting in the 'dan with his girlfriend, grousing that his own big ol' sedan could run better than those things out there.

"Prove it."

"I don't have any dough for the entry."

"I got some." she said.

Later, after turning 92 MPH, Art left with the first of many, many trophies: one that was, "About this big," he smiles as he holds his hands up like he's holding a pack of smokes!

Top: Good shot of Art finessing #25 at the Chrisman garage in Compton. This is pre-Hemi and post-stretch. A wonderful car, fully restored now, a tribute to the frontrunners of the day.

Center: We are very big fans of the #25 before the stretch, and the idea that is had an assortment of four bangers in it, the V8 flathead and finally a Hemi, kind of the symbol of engine choice evolution to that time. It can be traced as a racing hot rod back into the early 30s, maybe one of the most important hot rods of all time, we're thinkin'.

Above: Famous #25 in its only humbling form, before restoration and after a long look at making it a slingshot. We're glad it didn't work out!

Left: Little-known custom side of Art Chrisman demonstrates good taste in his first street car. Had "...about a hundred coats of maroon lacquer, sanded with 400 and gasoline." Packard taillights, everything molded, lowered spare, hot V8 and a Columbia butt. Asked, "How'd a poor, young guy get so much cool stuff on his first car?" Art says, "Worked and did it all myself."

Then you'll see the picture of #25 all dismantled in the shop. When was that?

"After Great Bend in '57 we cut it in half to make a slingshot out of it. Had to move the driver way out back and it just looked like shit. So I pushed it aside and built the Hussler."

#25 was next up on all four when it was restored.

So look this stuff over and savor it like we did and see if you can't find an opportunity to ask Art Chrisman a question. And get ready to grin.

There's a book in there somewhere, ain't there?

en hopup veritas

Above left: Harold Miller track roadster (this is what one is) had a Chrisman-owned flattie in it. Look at that low full-fendered model A with Deuce shell in the background. "They weren't low in the old days," you say? HA!

Left: Seen before, this is an important shot, since it clearly shows the Hop Up connection back in the day, which – we think – continues today. Mr. Chrisman thinks so.

Family fun in progress. The coupe is an avant-garde styling exercise, driven by streamlining requirements to achieve performance goals. It had a weird life after Chrisman, but it came home for restoration to the prime, most perfect state of its evolution.

T'n'A

Well, it doesn't have t' be a **banger** to be in here. No, it just has to be the recently neglected Ford Model T and Model A. There was a spell there where our guys lost them in favor of fat fendered sedans with velour chairs and carpet wrapped around their tilt steering columns. But somehow, the younger set (probably poverty working here) discovered them (Ts and As) and the appropriate exploitation is back on.

That, then, makes the earlier use of the skinny, wobbly things **nostalgic** to us. We get to revisit our roots in this chapter and see where the gag really got hooked up. Find out the who and how of the beginnings. Yeah. Turn the page for a gaggle of **gow.**

Hop Up Honor. *Stay Honor.*

Photo: Herbert Blomquest

Exhumed

HOLY SEPULCHER!

By Hop Up Staff – Photos by Drew Hardin

Back in Hop Up Volume II "The Golden Anniversary," we sneak-peeked a shot of the Ray Vega cover car from 1952. It's nearly done at the hands of Tony Handler, its long time caretaker. Well, ya might not call it caretaking if you heard some of the stories we heard over the years – know-what-I-mean?!

Some peripheral stories, though, had touched on this modified he'd had since he was 14. He'd street raced it with a 3/8 x 3/8 flathead – sneaking out of the bedroom window late at night and haunting the older cruisers on the streets of Beverly Hills. There's a hundred more tales and then, after it was owned for years by a best friend and

returned to Tony upon the passing of the friend, there's the saga of the mowed-down mailbox in the big hedge in the up-scale Santa Barbara neighborhood in...the 90s!!! That one appears to have been influenced by the use of an alternate fuel - know-what-I-mean?

We might call it growin' old gracefully...or not...

After the hedgecapade the rig was parked but never really forgotten. Tony knew right where it was all the time; but he'd been distracted with Rolls, Bentleys (how he makes a living) the Vega car, the other roadster in the shed...ya know? It came time to revive the Mod an' he says, "Hey Morty, ya wanna

Opposite page: She's got a nice butt. Symmetrical appointments, BH plate frame. Chrome wheels betray a period of 'inattention' to tradition but, hey. They ain't all that bad and the rubber is right in there.

Top: This entombment was only six or eight years old, but nature has a way of adding mystery to anything sitting kinda outside that long.

Above: Hollywood couldn't do the cobwebs as good as nature has.

Above right: The last caretaker spent time to suicide the front end. We think that was a good move; it stretched the wheelbase, lowered 'er, sexed 'er up a little bit.

Below right: Dash is a typical gow deal with lots of gook and goo. There's Antique Nationals placcques, neat switches, levers and knobs. Appointments. This kind of accessorizing was more popular back then..sometimes lead to gook wagon aesthetic. But this one stays on the correct side of that obvious line!

Below: The *Devil's Inn* the details.

come over and help me pull this thing out of it's slumber?"

"Oh Yeah," says Morty.

Reminiscent of the Lukkari Ardun Mod and the Freddie Rowe A rpu with a V8 flathead, this iteration of the little gow job has a model A banger in it with two pot Zephyr intake, and a feisty cam of unknown provenance.

After a battery, some ether, and some "Come-own, Baby" it started and ran, but had a clank inside that sounded like something in there was trying to get out. Since the noise was an unfamiliar one to Tony – and took him quite by surprise – we think the hurt part may have been a result of the ride that got the car in to the hedge with the mailbox.

Discretion dictated that we settle for a ride in the A-V8 you see in the background here rather than risk the obvious with the banger.

This page: Banger ran OK, but had been wounded. Blow by and a clankin' suggested something in there was 'tryin' to get out.' Owner scratched his head, recalling the last ride the thing was on and accepted blame for the apparent wounds.

It's Only A...
Model A Sport Coupe

By Norman Pearson Marchment

Or Is It ?

Just out of the service after the war in '46, I returned home to find my mom had sold my '32 three window for me (Dumb! But who knew.) while I was overseas, leaving me with no wheels. Money was as scarce as new cars, and one doesn't do much with the income from the GI Bill.

A friend of mine, Jim, needed to sell his '31 Sport Coupe, as his new bride was expecting their first child. The car wasn't much. Bright green brush paint job, black stock top. The only thing not stock were four terrible 16" wheels and different headlights. Everything else was stock, 4 banger, updraft carb, everything. Just married myself, I gave up our last $200 and it became mine-all mine. (Ours. "Jinx" and me.)

Sometime later, a friend suggested I turn my "A" into an AV8 and gave me a tired '37 Ford flathead.

That started many years of work, enjoyment, expense and learning. The things I learned enabled me to be successful at a career I loved, aviation. Having never done an engine swap or welding before, it was quite a challenge. When I finished the first phase the "A" was an AV8 with Trans, hydraulic brakes, '32 shell and grill.

It never occurred to me to build a "Hot Rod." This was my daily driver and work car, and it had the usual problems. So I took my radiator apart and built about a 2 gallon upper tank out of brass. I'd love to say that solved the problem. It didn't. It only delayed the overheating. I still run the same radiator.

The powertrain and running gear were eventually upgraded to a hopped up 59AB backed by a Lincoln trans, and then was time to continue upgrading the rest of the car. I Z'd the rear frame for a '48 rear end with 4:11 gears, '48 brakes all around, safety hubs on axles, telescopic shocks, dropped front axle, clothespin radius rods, and cross over steering. Front spring was lowered and had turned eyes. Wasn't much more I could do. It seemed like a lot of work for a "driver," especially when I had to do most things myself. The top came off next. Jinx and I laminated new oak bows and replaced all of the wood components. The center bow was lowered, and we installed fiberglass sheets to form a poor man's "Carson" top. The cowl gas tank was cut and filled to allow new instruments on the new dash panel...top swing pedals and dual master cylinders on the firewall for brakes and a hydraulic actuated clutch. Gas tank was placed in rumble seat compartment. The center hinge was cut out of the hood top which was welded together and piano-hinged to the stock louvered side panels. I made up my own latch system (it worked but not easily). Changed over to 12V and rewired all. Had glass packs with the exit ahead of the rear wheels. (Just too hard to get tail pipes thru all that mess back there.) Black Naugahyde tuck and roll

with white acoustical headliner. A beautiful teal colored lacquer, Firestone treads, and, wow, she was something.

By 1963, I got things a little too thin on my engine. I love onramps to freeways. Over did it one too many times and blew up my pride and joy. A rod let go and almost cut the poor thing in half. I really felt bad about that and so did Jinx. Obviously we needed a new car. So we bought a Chevy wagon and a spare engine for the coupe. Out came the 59AB and in went a 283. I must say I was surprised. While not as strong, it was smooth, sounded pretty good, stayed much cooler, and I didn't have to keep trying to adjust the carbs. Big change, but I missed her flattie's radical sound, polished aluminum and muscle.

Let's move the clock ahead many years, happy as they were. In July of 1997, I started reactivating the "A" and realized a nice 350 would make more sense than my 283. After looking at all the magazines, going to car shows etc., I got carried away with upgrading the car. We went all out and started assembling the parts needed to renew "our baby." A new TCI frame, dropped tube front axle, Currie

rear end, discs in front, all the goodies, and lots of chrome. A great 357, (computer dyno 400 hp) chrome wheels and new Goodrich tires.

In the summer of 2006, I had my niece and her husband over for dinner. Tom took one look at my "A" and said, "Uncle Norm, don't touch it, don't touch anything. Not the paint, not the engine, nothing." Those were words I couldn't understand, as the new chassis with all the trimmings was sitting right next to my coupe. He said in a friendly way, but forcefully, that if I changed her now I would be destroying a true early homebuilt hot rod. I had to agree, as no one except me has ever done much to her other than aligning the front end.

Sometime after that I called Tom because I needed some more room for a project I was working on and wanted to know if he could store the "A" and the new chassis. With the landscaping projects and the new deck I was building on the house I put the "A" on the back burner once again. A couple of months went by and Tom called. He said, "Come pick up your coupe, Uncle Norm, cause she's up and running and ready to be a part of our family again."

One thing I know for sure...

She's not for sale.

Opposite top: Clean interior with a host of SW gauges and a '40 wheel.

Opposite center: Old fuel log hints at the 3X2 set up that once lived on a hot flathead.

Opposite bottom: The stance is just perfect in this 3⁄4 rear shot.

Above: Running the slalom course at Riverside Raceway.

Right and below: Norm and his model A in the late 50s and now. Two hot rod survivors still together...

Swanky T

The Story of Heggie's T Roadster

by Marc D'Estout - Photos by Mike Narciso

Vallejo, CA based Swanx member Anji Ramsey was driven, obsessed. She had to retrieve a family heirloom that had slipped away, for several years, to an "outsider." The object of her desire was Heggie's T. You see, "Heggie" was grandpa Marlin Hegendeffer, and that 1927 Ford hot rod T was a childhood memory that she couldn't shake.

The T had actually passed hands through several family members over a few decades, and fortunately the car had quite a history

in the Nor Cal area, so tracking it down only took a couple of years...of intense sleuthing.

The traceable history begins in the early 1940s when the car was owned by Paul Wordig. Shortly before WWII, Wordig Z'd the frame, channeled the body, updated the suspension etc., and since he collected aircraft engines, the original V8 for this gow job was not made by Henry or Cadillac, but by the legendary Hispano Suiza Co. This is one of the earliest examples of a V8, the

Opposite: This is a real survivor. What appears to be a black roadster is actually a deep purple. Extensive chrome is mostly original.

Above: Heggie's chrome work can be seen here on...well almost everything except body, tank and frame.

Below: And you thought importing V8s from France was a new thing. This "Hisso," possibly from a French Spad, could produce 200 hp. Note chroming on front end had begun already by the time this vintage image was taken.

same engine used in WWI French Spads and British SE5s. These OHC V8s could produce 200 hp. Talk about gow!

Around 1947 Heggie, who ran a chrome plating shop in Vallejo, acquired the modified roadster from Wordig in trade for plating work on some of Wordig's motorcycle projects. Shortly after acquisition, Heggie proceeded to make the T his own. He stripped the car, boxed the frame with 1/4" plate, and added substantial chrome treatments to just about every part of the chassis, including lever shocks, dog bones, springs etc. He also added chrome-reversed rims, back when ya had t' make 'em yourself. Not only was it a personalized effort, but the treatment also served as a rolling advertisement for Heggie's plating shop. It's not clear what happened to

the Hisso mill, but one of Henry's V8s soon found its way into the now gleaming chrome chassis.

Family stories recount Heggie's racing history; mostly at the local circle tracks with his "hardtops," but stories also include racing

Top row left to right: Heggie even chromed the custom made dash, photo circa 1949.

A friend helps as progress begins on more extensive modifications, chrome banjo rear can be seen here under the seriously Z'd frame.

Heggie, standing, works on the "new" flathead with helper.

Hoisted and ready to drop in: note chrome bell housing and oil pan along with front end hardware.

Above: Heggie in jacket, has back to camera. Another uncle, Ray Schultz, shown in photo on ground helping prep car, circa 1950.

the T at both dry lakes and Nor Cal drag strips. The collection of trophies bestowed upon the car, however, was largely from local shows...like "The Oakland Roadster Show"! It was also featured in the September 1950 Hot Rod magazine looking much as it does today.

"Uncle" Rick Pilling took possession of the T in 1958 and, turns out, was an original member of the Swanx. The T, along with "Uncle Rick" and "Aunt Ilene," soon found themselves on the cover of the July 1959 Rod Builder & Customizer magazine. Around 1963 Heggie got his hands on the car again and made additional modifications that included an OHV Cad mill and S.C.o.T blower, installed with the assistance of Anji's dad, George Ramsey. Heggie passed away in '68, and Anji's uncle Tommy (Tommy Gill) acquired the car. Tommy replaced Heggie's deep purple paint with a typically wild 60s paint job and swapped the all chrome banjo rear end with a newly chromed '55 Chevy rear. (Grandma now ran the plating shop, so chrome was still an affordable treatment.) The car was reintroduced at shows and picked up even more trophies well into the early 70s. But this is where the T goes AWOL... In 1972, just before Tommy Gill passed away, the T was sold outside the family and essentially "disappeared" until Anji began tracking it down in the mid 90s.

Anji found Heggie's T in 1997 stashed away in a garage up in California Gold Country. After two years of negotiating, she finally bought the car in 1999. Here's where the project became a team effort between Anji's family and her fellow Swanx club members. Gunar Hansken of the Swanx was the primary builder of the car, bringing it to its current state. Other Swanx members lent a hand in the restoration, too. Anji's dad, (who also owned the "family car" for a brief time) helped wrench and helped finance the project.

The car was eventually re-fitted with a freshly built 239 flathead from a '52 Ford, topped with a very early cut-down Thickston intake and a set of vintage Edmunds heads supplied by a cousin. Anji and Gunar found and installed a couple of 97s and labored

over details. The new handmade exhaust replicated Heggie's flathead exhaust as close as possible. After much research, the T was repainted back to deep "Packard Purple" at Manuel's Auto Body in Vallejo, and a couple of tired parts were then re-chromed...at considerable more cost than before! Most of the chrome, however, is "50s original" from Heggie's shop. To finish the restoration, the period perfect upholstery was carefully recreated by Able, also at Manuel's.

In 2006 the "Swanky Family T" made its restored debut at BilletProof and, shortly after, The San Francisco Rod & Custom Show. This heirloom will certainly remain in the family for a little longer.

Hop Up Honor ... oh yea!

Right: The T in 1963 configuration with blown Cad mill.

Following page, clockwise from top: Upholstery is buttoned in, as Heggie's original was, so it could be switched for different looks. Original rumored to still be in a Vallejo garage.

Ross box seen here poking out of pleated firewall. Gotta love that!

Profile shows nice balance and how low they could go back then.

Front end; all chrome from here.

Acknowledgments

This is kinda like saying Grace before a meal, only **after**. There's certainly somebody to thank, like contributors, staff, car owners, readers...and we do that regularly.

Without getting into the likelihood of there being a 'Hot Rod Deity,' we can at least agree that there is an aura, something mystical about this preoccupation we have; there's a compelling presence among us that ain't some Ed Winfield type in robes or anything. Rather, it's a sense of what is right **to us** in the expression of life with trad hot rods and customs.

We want to acknowledge that the spirit–that's it–is with us, and we are gratified that it brings us together. And since this is the **Tabernacle of Gow**, say "Halleluiah, Brutha. Halleluiah."

It's About the Iron.

Photo: Herbert Blomquest